LIFE WITH A
sprinkle of
glitter

DISCARDED

LIFE WITH A
sprinkle of
glitter

Louise Pentland

SIMON &
SCHUSTER

London · New York · Sydney · Toronto · New Delhi

A CBS COMPANY

First published in Great Britain by Simon & Schuster UK Ltd, 2015
A CBS company

1 3 5 7 9 10 8 6 4 2

Simon & Schuster UK Ltd
1st Floor
222 Gray's Inn Road
London WC1X 8HB

www.simonandschuster.co.uk

Simon & Schuster Australia, Sydney

Simon & Schuster India, New Delhi

A CIP catalogue record for this book is available from
the British Library

Hardback ISBN: 978-1-4711-4972-6
eBook ISBN: 978-1-4711-4973-3

Design and illustrations by Corinna Farrow

Printed and bound in Italy by L.E.G.O. S.p.A.

Dedication

"My very first book
is dedicated lovingly
to the two most
important women in my
life, my wonderful
mother and my
sweet daughter."

Inside

Aloha Sprinklerinos! 8

GLITZ   12-77
Beauty and Pampering   14
Partying   32
Meeting Celebrities   46
The Art of Shopping   52
Travelling in Style   64

CREATE   78-131
Setting Up Home   80
Prettifying Your Room   92
Crafts   108
Anti-Baking   122

NEED TO KNOWS   132–201

Surviving Education	134
Bullying	152
Online Safety	160
Body Confidence	176
Comfort Zones	190

ALL ABOUT LOVE   202–251

Boys and Lurve	204
Dating	218
Bonding with Baby	230
Being Kind	240

Toodlepip!	252
Thank yous	254
Picture Credits	256

Aloha Sprinklerinos!

I lead a happy life.
What a marvellous first line for the first page of my first book.
I lead a very happy life.

I lead a happy life because I choose to. I choose to fill my days and my mind with good people, kind thoughts and positive experiences. Naturally, just like every other little soul out there, I have the days that are dark and dreary and I encounter experiences that I wouldn't want to treasure forever, but I choose to deal with them in such a way that they do not put a dent in my joy. I choose my life.

In the last ten years, my life has gone from depressing and frightening to gorgeous and glamorous, and after sharing my experiences on my blog and YouTube channels, I wanted to take the next step and write a book. Not an autobiography (I've still got so much living to do!), but a guide to taking yourself from bad to good, or from good to great. A guide to adding positivity into every area of your life, whether it's as big as your very best friend or as tiny as the things you display on your dressing table – all these things matter.

Happiness is not measured in size but in significance. The trinkets I have dotted around my home matter as much to my well-being as the nights I have out with my friend Clare, who usually orders one too many cocktails and dances on velvet sofas. All happy things, all worth noting.

Imagine you are in one of those glorious vintage shops where every surface is laden with treasure. Cut glass, pill boxes, old cameras, pendants, chests of drawers and stacks and stacks of books. This book is like that. **Each chapter is one of those gem-encrusted tins that you can open, peep inside and enjoy.** You can either methodically wander the entire shop, looking at each item in order, or you can dance around with wild abandon, opening and closing whatever you like, whenever you like, and enjoying the contents at your leisure. This book is for you to consume and enjoy. You can take in tiny bits of it at a time or you can devour it all in one go. I don't mind. I don't mind how you go about it; all that matters to me is that you take something from it.

I want you to walk away from this book and feel uplifted. I want you to feel as though you are equipped to deal with something in your life and deal with it in the best possible, positive way. I want you to feel as happy as I do.

I'm not saying that to be sickeningly twee or to feel superior to anyone, I say it from experience. I have felt what they call 'rock bottom'. I have felt that very desperate sadness that hits you when you need it least

and when you feel so far from love and joy that you can't quite recall what they felt like in the first place. I know that, in those times, it's a very tall mountain to climb to choose happiness.

This is not a pity party; this was the first chapter of my life. It was called 'childhood'. I grew up in a happy, affluent, suburban family with a stay-at-home mother, businessman father and an array of local children to play outside with. We had a lovely house, a pet hamster called Celeste and a swing in the back garden. It was idyllic.

When I was five, my mother was diagnosed with cancer and our lives were shattered. She fought bravely for two years, undergoing treatment after treatment, losing her beautiful hair, the use of her body and eventually her life. It was devastating. Nobody should have to watch their mummy die in such a slow and drawn-out way, and her passing left a huge hole in my heart.

It was a horrid time in my life and as I entered my early teens things at home were incredibly difficult, for a number of reasons that I won't go into here. In that period, I experienced what it is that the bottom really feels like. But from it I learnt an important lesson, which is that things won't always feel that bad. Having survived all that pain and come out on the other side of it, I gained a sense of perspective that many people have to work on for years to achieve. Lucky me.

I've done it though. Not by magic, but by addressing each area of my life and having a serious think about my attitude.

Something I talk about a lot (and I mean a lorra lorra lot) on my blog is changing the way we think. A lady I once knew used to say, 'The mind is a very powerful thing, Louise', and she wasn't wrong. Your eyes might be your window to the world but your mind is the power station where everything is processed and worked out. Your mind can control your moods, your moods can control your actions and your actions have big consequences on you and those around you.

You can choose to have a mind that finds the good in things or that offers love and support, or you can choose something else. There are times when it feels like there are no choices or that all the choices are bad ones, but this isn't the case. We simply have to look at things in a specific way to really see what we are looking for – happiness.

Happiness is there for everyone. There are no limits or quotas. You can't buy it, or trade it, or earn it. You just choose it.

I hope that by exploring topics like comfort zones, beauty and pampering, setting up home, and boys and love, I can show you how I find so much joy and enrichment in my life and how you can too.

Louise Pentland

Glitz

Beauty and Pampering 14

PARTYING 32

MEETING CELEBRITIES 46

The Art of Shopping 52

Travelling in Style 64

Beauty and Pampering

> Beauty is in the eye of the beholder
>
> BEAUTY IS ONLY SKIN DEEP
>
> Beauty shines from within

We've all heard these sayings and we probably all agree, but that doesn't mean a gal (or guy, for that matter) doesn't want to take care of themselves and enjoy a pamper session here and there.

I want to share all my little tips and tricks, stories and insights on that big ol' topic of beauty, pampering and cosmetics. I'm no expert, but after spending five years writing a beauty blog, I've started collecting a good few titbits here and there that I'd love to share!

Pampering

Let's start with the big stuff: pampering.

Pampering, to me, is the base of beauty. Your hair and make-up are always going to look dewier, brighter and shinier if you've spent some time pouring your tender loving care into it. There are plenty of pampering options to suit any budget or taste, but here are a few of my personal favourites.

Spas

Oh me oh my, the ultimate place to go for any pampered gal about town (which, incidentally, is the name of a gorgeous MAC lipstick shade, but more on that later). The soft hues, the gentle sound of wind chimes, the subtle smell of eucalyptus and the soothing voices of the beauty therapists – it's enough to make anyone relax into an aromatherapy-induced slumber.

For those of you not in the know, a spa is a place to go for all manner of body treatments, ranging from hot stone massages to body wraps, and pedicures to facials. Each spa will have an enticing little menu (either online or when you walk in) of delicious experiences you can have, aimed at rejuvenating, relaxing or improving various areas of your body. Spas can be dedicated stand-alone buildings, incorporated into the facilities at a hotel (some hotels of course are there purely for the use of the spa), available as extras to enjoy at gyms or even tucked away in first-class lounges at airports.

Relaxing is serious business.

Get it right. Be sure to arrive a few minutes early so you have time to fill out the forms they give you (don't worry, you won't be signing your life away, more just ticking boxes about your skin type or any allergies you have), slip into a fluffy robe and familiarise yourself with the surroundings. As well as factoring in time beforehand, consider blocking time out for afterwards too. If you've just spent 60 minutes in a state of oily bliss (oh my), your perfectly pampered body won't appreciate being rushed off and forced back into your busy life. Allow yourself to take things slowly and accept that a little bit of luxury and you time is important.

A lot of spas actually have a sort of 'pre-treatment' area for you to unwind a little bit in. Last year, I was in Seattle visiting my friend Marie (YouTuber Bitsandclips) and we decided to leave the babies with their daddies and head to the spa for the afternoon. We were already a bit giddy at the prospect of child-free pampering but by the time we were sat in the artfully darkened room, listening to whale song, we were almost delirious. Marie was handed a cup of berry tea and I nibbled on a 'Luna Bar', which just tickled me further because it said on the wrapper that it was to 'replace what you lose each month', and so all manner of crude jokes were made. Essentially, we were two grown women, giggling and rolling about the place for no real reason, but the fact that we were supposed to remain calm and quiet made it even worse! Do you ever get that? Where you are supposed to be super serious but that makes everything oh so hysterical?

Something I hear a lot of people mention when I talk about spas is a feeling of awkwardness with the beauty therapists. I get it. I've been there. I've felt that painful shyness as some very soothing but still very unknown lady glides her hands round my shoulders. Should you make small talk? Should you apologise excessively for silly things like your hair being in the way or your legs having the tiniest bit of stubble? Should you speak up if you don't like the treatment? Should you keep your underwear on? All these worries can create a mountain of panic and, trust me, I've been there!

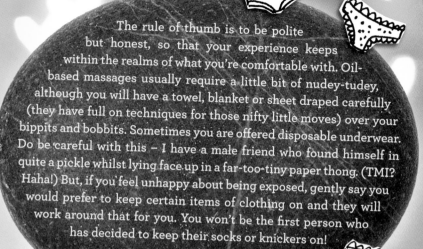

The rule of thumb is to be polite but honest, so that your experience keeps within the realms of what you're comfortable with. Oil-based massages usually require a little bit of nudey-tudey, although you will have a towel, blanket or sheet draped carefully (they have full on techniques for those nifty little moves) over your bippits and bobbits. Sometimes you are offered disposable underwear. Do be careful with this – I have a male friend who found himself in quite a pickle whilst lying face up in a far-too-tiny paper thong. (TMI? Haha!) But, if you feel unhappy about being exposed, gently say you would prefer to keep certain items of clothing on and they will work around that for you. You won't be the first person who has decided to keep their socks or knickers on!

If any state of undress at all perturbs you, opt for a treatment that requires no nudity, like a facial or reiki. Similarly, ring and ask ahead of time if any of the massages are suitable to have clothed. I once had a wonderful neck and shoulder massage in the Heathrow Airport Cowshed Spa with all my clothes on, which was quite a blessing since my dad was there having one too! Bottom line is, the staff at spas want you to feel as good as possible, so they will go with whatever you feel is best to make the experience perfect.

👑 **A top tip to eliminate any anxieties you might have:**
Before going, make sure you are fresh and happy with yourself (I always make sure to shave and moisturise my legs, remove all my make-up if I'm having a facial, etc.) and remember that the therapists have seen every sort of body and every kind of person, so you will not stand out or be anything unusual to them. Leave your worries at home and let yourself slip off into a happy bliss.

Beauty Treatments

👑 **A top tip if spa days are a bit too much of a splurge for you: consider treating yourself to a one-off beauty treatment every now and again.** Since being filmed and photographed is a big part of my job, I am pretty good at keeping myself in tippy-top condition beauty-wise (let's not discuss exercise here – eep) and have regular manicures and trips to the hair salon.

If you are pushed for time and pennies, my biggest tip for you would be to book yourself a blow out at your local hair salon. For one whole hour, you can sit in peace (a huge luxury if you have little ones at home, a busy job or a heavy workload), have your hair washed, enjoy a head massage, sit and play on your phone, read a magazine or sip a coffee. Some salons will even offer you a glass of bubbly whilst a professional transforms you into a swishy-haired goddess. I make sure to give myself this hour every single week (shhh, it's essential!), and for £18.50 a pop it is so, so worth it. The hairstyle lasts a good few days, my calm mood lasts a good few hours and, since I have built up such a great relationship with my stylist, I know I can trust her to make me feel fabulous.

The same goes for manicures and pedicures.
Find a nail technician you gel with (see the
pun? Heh), and visit regularly. You'll reach a
lovely point where not only are you having
an hour of beautifying, but you're also having
an hour with a friend to chat, laugh and feel
lovely on the inside as well as the outside.

Try these
colours
on your
nails

Home Pampering

Saying all that, solo pampering might be more up your alley and I have plenty to say on that too!

When I used to work a very long and very boring 9–5 (more like 8–6.30, urgh) office job, before the days of blogs and babies, I used to regularly set aside a 'beauty night'. I would keep the whole evening free of social plans, run a bubble bath, drop a Lush bath bomb in, light candles, set my laptop up on the laundry hamper with a DVD running (be VERY careful with this – the bathroom is a risky place for electronics, obviously!) and just soak. It would be the perfect time to exfoliate skin, shave legs, remove chipped nail polish, file, base coat, paint and top coat said nails, apply a face mask, deep condition hair, pluck brows and, once out of the bubbly depths, moisturise and fake tan. A. Lot. Of. Pampering.

If you're going to do something, do it well.
I would spend at least two hours doing all of
this and then the next day would strut into my
office feeling like a king amongst men, except,
yanno, a lady amongst mostly other ladies. It
didn't matter. The point was, I'd spent relaxing
time, with myself, for myself, and that's
something a lot of us neglect to do.

It is so easy to put evenings like that off in
favour of looking after our families, meeting
deadlines or seeing friends. I'm not suggesting
you jump ship and abandon all responsibilities
to paint your nails and watch the next episode of
Mad Men on Netflix (which I highly recommend
by the way), but take a night once in a while to
really spend focusing on yourself and having a
little pamper binge – you'll feel amazing for it.

**If absolutely none of the above are things you think you can
achieve or work into your life, do two simple things at least,
and your body will thank you.**

❧ *Drink plenty of water (2 litres a day is recommended)*

❧ *Allow yourself enough sleep*

If you feel you are slacking in either of those areas, set yourself
little challenges to achieve your goal. Rather than going all out
and making huge life changes right away, consider upping your
water intake by just a couple of glasses a day or snuggling into
your duvet half an hour earlier than usual. With little alterations
you can make big differences to your overall well-being, and who
doesn't want to look bright eyed and bushy tailed? I know I do.

Skincare

Next on the beauty list is skincare. Some people love spending time on their skin, whilst others find it quite the chore. Although I think I might be in Team Chore, I realise it is pretty important and therefore spend quite a lot of time on it.

Why is it important Louise? It's so boring. Yeah, I know. Removing make-up and daily grime from pollutants and goodness knows what else isn't exactly thrilling but, without it, your skin is going to go downhill fast. Even if you aren't applying make-up each day, those little skin cells are dying (as they are supposed to) and you are walking around in pollution, with all kinds of germs and nasties that need to be washed away each and every day. If you are wearing make-up, that obviously needs to be removed too.

For a long time, I used make-up wipes. You know, those little wet wipes in pastel-coloured packets that are oh so easy to use and oh so convenient. I mentioned this to a skincare expert friend of mine, Caroline Hirons, and she was aghast! 'Make-up wipes are for flights, fannies and festivals!' she said. 'Would you stop giving Baby Glitter baths and only use wet wipes on her?' 'No,' I answered. She had made her point.

I spent hours researching blog posts and testing facial products and eventually found a system that I really enjoy and that works wonders. My skin has thanked me and I have thanked Caroline. The make-up wipe manufacturers have cried over lost sales. Well, maybe not.

Skincare systems vary from person to person. Some folk go for the lazy make-up wipe route (as discussed, I once lived there), some have a simple three-step system (my new home) and some have a more complex routine (I hope to graduate here soon). I shan't spend too much time on this topic because I'm not the expert, but I'll share with you my habits and then point you in the right direction if you are looking for more help or information.

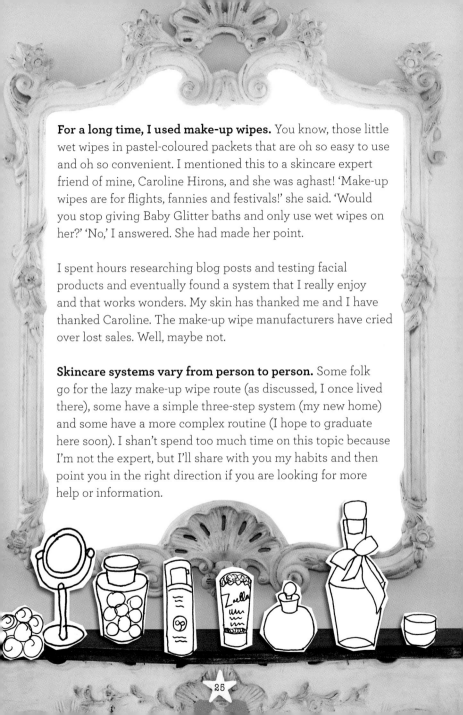

Cleansing

I wear make-up at least four to five days a week, as well as trotting around London, so my skin needs a good deal of cleansing at the end of my day. I flit between the Liz Earle Cleanse and Polish Hot Cloth Cleanser or the Emma Hardie Moringa Cleansing Balm. You massage the cream (for Liz Earle) or balm (for Emma Hardie) into dry, dirty (ew) skin and then, with a warm, damp cloth, remove all the yuk. It feels incredible. There is something so satisfying about watching all your make-up kind of dissolve into the remover products and then taking a lovely clean cloth and swiping it all away.

Toning

I spent a good many months toning but not knowing what it was. One day, I curiously asked on Twitter and was met with a barrage of responses telling me it is to tighten your pores and remove any traces of dirt left over from step one. Fair enough, I'll carry on then. I have enjoyed the Lush Eau Roma Water Toner but find myself repeat-buying the Liz Earle Instant Boost Skin Tonic bottle. It seems like such a trivial little step but I find if I do miss it, I notice the difference when it's time to apply make-up. I feel like it sits better when the skin has been toned. A sneaky little step not to be dismissed.

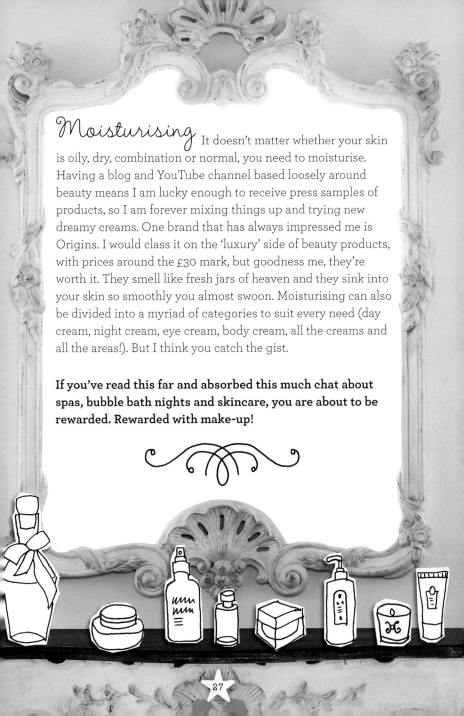

Moisturising

It doesn't matter whether your skin is oily, dry, combination or normal, you need to moisturise. Having a blog and YouTube channel based loosely around beauty means I am lucky enough to receive press samples of products, so I am forever mixing things up and trying new dreamy creams. One brand that has always impressed me is Origins. I would class it on the 'luxury' side of beauty products, with prices around the £30 mark, but goodness me, they're worth it. They smell like fresh jars of heaven and they sink into your skin so smoothly you almost swoon. Moisturising can also be divided into a myriad of categories to suit every need (day cream, night cream, eye cream, body cream, all the creams and all the areas!). But I think you catch the gist.

If you've read this far and absorbed this much chat about spas, bubble bath nights and skincare, you are about to be rewarded. Rewarded with make-up!

Cosmetics

To me, cosmetics are the icing on the cake of beauty. It's the fun, the art and the glamour of pampering. Get it right and you can feel a million dollars. Get it wrong and all you need do is remove it and start over. It's frivolous, easy and totally your call. I'm utterly in love with it.

I sense that if you are reading this chapter, you probably have a basic grasp of make-up so I will refrain from boring you with the basics. Instead, I'm going to share with you some of my favourite tips and tricks to keep in mind next time you delve into your make-up bag.

◎ Apply a primer

This is quite a new lesson learnt for me, but I have found time and time again that spending the extra twenty seconds on a base layer makes all the difference later into the day, when your face is still the way you wanted it to be eight hours ago. I enjoy a silicone-based primer by Benefit POREfessional; I apply it with my fingers for speed and ease, and I make sure to remove it thoroughly at night to prevent skin breakouts and spots. By applying a primer, you are helping to fill in pores, fine lines and uneven areas, and this allows your foundation to sit better on the face and achieves a more flawless look. It seems boring but, trust me, it makes a difference!

✳ Slow and steady wins the race with foundation

It's often tempting to be heavy handed with your foundation (especially if it is liquid) because we all want that completely flawless look, non? Well proceed with caution here. Apply a thin layer with a clean brush and see how you look. Then, if you feel you need more, apply another layer. The point is, build up small, gentle layers rather than swirling a goopy mess around your face. You'll avoid unsightly brush strokes and lessen wastage. Another golden rule: blend into your neck and under the chin. Foundation tide lines are a huge no-no!

✒ Wash your brushes

I have a friend (who shall remain anonymous, for fear of her swiftly un-friending me) who once confessed to never having washed her make-up brushes. 'It's fine,' she said, 'nobody uses them except me, so it's only my germs.' Wrong, my little petite pois. This is not how it works. Your brushes are a breeding ground for bacteria and other nasties. If they are being used for liquid or cream products, then even more so. Give them regular washes with warm water and a gentle shampoo (I use my daughter's), or you can buy specialist brush cleansers too. I'm not suggesting you go gaga and dash to the bathroom after every use (although hats off to you if you do), but keep in mind that any yukkies that form on your brush will then be transferred to your delicate skin – no thank you!

✤ Be bold with colour

Something I struggled with for years was being brave with colours.
I found myself sticking to browns, golds and pinks, and whilst they
all have their merits, every once in a while it's fun to branch out and
try a super-bright lip colour (MAC, Illamasqua and Rimmel all have
a very wide selection of shades) or be dramatic with eyeshadows. If
you are stuck for inspiration, turn to YouTube. There are hundreds of
thousands of amazing tutorials out there to help out.

♡ Lip liner is your friend

Kind of like the primer tip, this is one of those that takes a teeny bit
of time for a whole heap of reward. Lip liner allows you to more easily
create a really professional lip look, without the lipstick smudging or
bleeding as much. It's especially worthwhile if you are taking on board
my previous tip of branching out with colours.

✿ Bright eyes

To make your eyes look a little bigger and wider (think Disney
Princess kinda dealio), apply a little bit of white, ivory, gold or pale
pink eyeshadow to the inner corner of the lid (next to your tear duct)
and a little bit under the outer half of your eyebrow. This will create an
illusion of space and voilà, instantly larger peepers!

Ooooeeeee that was a lorra lorra beauty chat. I feel so ready to jump into a deep bubble bath and preen myself all day!

Something I'd like to finish up on is accepting your beauty. We've all heard the phrases I mentioned at the start of this chapter, and I think very often we dismiss them in favour of applying some fake tan and curling our locks, but I wanted to take a moment to focus on accepting that we are beautiful.

Yes, it is the most fun to apply make-up and paint our nails, but they are only added extras. If you spend a moment looking at the human face or body, it's so perfect. Next time you have a moment, go and look in a mirror and before you find something to criticise or worry about, note how incredible your eyes are, or delight in the lines of your body and know that there is nothing wrong with you. There is nothing 'not nice' about any of us. All too often the media, society or just our own internal critic tells us that there are parts of our bodies or faces that do not reach a certain standard of beauty. This is utter rubbish.

Who decides what is beautiful? Is there one person in charge of this? Is there a set-in-stone list of rules for what a person must look like to be gorgeous? Nope. It's just us. Each and every one of us is the decider.

Decide you are beautiful, and you are.

PARTYING

For as long as I can remember, I have loved parties. There is something so magical about so many people coming together to focus on a happy occasion. Where people only do enjoyable things and spend quality time with one another (no working or doing chores here, thank you kindly!). I would go as far as to say a party is my most favourite place to be.

Because my job is so social, my friendship circle has widened, which is great fun, and I seem to find myself at a lot of parties. There have been some parties where I have excelled, and there have been others where I've failed miserably (or hysterically, depending on which side you're watching from!). In this chapter, I'm going to tell you everything I know about handling a party. From invitation etiquette to getting home safely – this is the party guide for you!

Since we're gonna go into this, we may as well start from the beginning – it's a very good place to start (name that film reference). As a little girl, my mother would pull out all the stops to throw a classic at-home-1990s-children's-party. There'd be little girls in puff-sleeved dresses and little boys in smart trousers that would be instantly ruined by those oh so impressive knee skids we liked to do to Michael Jackson songs. There'd be chocolate fingers and party rings on paper plates, balloons and a party bag with a cheap toy and slice of cake wrapped in a napkin. It was perfect. It was what 6-year-old Louise lived for. It felt like every Saturday that I was being driven to a classmate's house, where I'd play musical chairs and eat so much jelly and ice cream that I'd feel sick in the car home. At one point, I remember my mum bulk-buying generic birthday gifts to give to all the little kiddies who invited me to their special days.

As I grew a little older, parties matured. I remember once a girl called Natasha held a 'Black and White Party' for her tenth birthday and, truly, I felt this was the most sophisticated event I had ever attended. There I was, coolly sipping Cherryade in the corner of the low-lit community centre, in black leggings, white crop top and – the pièce de résistance – my silver stick-on earrings, feeling like the cat who got the cream. Honestly, I strive to feel that great about myself at parties even now. As goodie bags, Natasha gave out tiny, oval Forever Friends tins with friendship bracelets in. That sealed it for me; she was the greatest 10-year-old I knew. She had it all. She had the theme sorted, she had the favours down and she had all the style. From then on, I knew I would forever strive for party perfection.

Now, if anyone knows how to throw a children's birthday party, it's my American friend Marie... Recently, her little boy Luca turned one and the lady deep fried her own cronuts (half croissant, half donut), to add to her 'Our Little Fox' woodland food theme. She had fox tails (sweet potato fries), fox holes (the hand-crafted cronuts) and of course a bevy of perfectly decorated foxy cakes. As if that wouldn't have made my mum (Mrs Biscuits on Paper Plates) envious enough, Marie hand-crafted a selection of decorations, including brown rustic favour bags, autumnal coloured bunting and party hats.

A great tip I learnt from Marie last year when she was prepping for her daughter Scarlet's birthday was to sprinkle your own version of your children's favourites. At the time, Scarlet was really into the classic cartoon character Strawberry Shortcake. She wanted Strawberry Shortcake eevverrytthhiinnggg. Like me, Marie wasn't a fan of the tacky-cartoon-faces-everywhere look, but she still wanted to throw a party they would both like. This is the point where I would have given up or given in. Not Marie. Not super-party-thrower extraordinaire Marie.

Instead of smattering her house with store-bought yuk, she took elements of Strawberry Shortcake and infused them into a shabby-chic, handmade theme. Lemonade cake with pink and red icing; pink, red and pale green paper party hats; pear-green jelly beans in pink paper cones for favours, and plenty of little hand-drawn pastel Strawberry Shortcakes to adorn everything with. It really was the sweetest affair, made all the sweeter by the time and work Marie had lovingly poured into the day for her baby girl. Love and craft wins out every time. If you are stuck for inspiration, take yourself off to Pinterest, where you will be met with a plethora of party ideas to thrill and excite! And don't be afraid to use your imagination and put your own personal spin on a theme.

As you move from your childhood into your teenage years, you are met with a myriad of challenges, including that all important area – night life. I think teen parties can be divided into several categories, including house, school or hosted at a venue. Each one comes with its own potential pitfalls, but each one can be successfully navigated if you have the knowhow. The party areas that really used to trip me up when I was a teenager were fashion, drinking, getting home and boys, boys, boys.

FASHION

The party experience would start with me at home, staring at my very untrendy wardrobe collection and wondering what I could wear to make me seem much cooler than I really was. With an assortment of items from Mark One and Tammy Girl, I usually found something to pull together, and considering it was the early 2000s (where handkerchief tops and lilac trousers were all the rage), I did OK. If in doubt, go for something simple with a hint of glitz. Better to go classic than crazy, I always think.

A little trick I use even now is to plan outfits in advance. Even if you have nowhere to go, have some items in your wardrobe that you know would work well for a birthday party or a night out. Just knowing they are there makes things a lot easier when it comes to putting a style together. For example, I have a black jersey dress in my cupboard and I know that if I throw on a gold belt and pair it with some heels, it looks great for every occasion. It's like a very glamorous 'break glass in case of emergency' situation.

DRINKING

Usually at the parents-are-on-holiday house parties, there would be a good deal of mismatched alcohol. No peach bellinis in those days, but mostly half bottles of liquor or cheap wine we'd pinched from our parents' stashes. Eep. My biggest piece of advice here is that if you are going to drink (and of course you should be sticking to your country's legal age limits), sip slowly. I often felt that I should be holding a drink as it gave me something to do with my hands and made me feel like I was fitting in (not really a good enough reason to drink, but certainly the truth of the matter). Rather than knocking drinks back and helping yourself to constant refills, sip slowly and make that drink last a long time. You really, really do not want to be a drunk mess and you absolutely don't want to lose sense of what you're doing. You can still have an amazing night without overdoing the drinks. At the risk of sounding boring, please know your limits and be sensible.

Stand strong on drinking. If you are offered a drink and you would prefer not to drink, just don't. I have been in many situations where friends would chant ('Drink! Drink! Drink!') or sing songs ('Down in onnnneee, you Zulu warrior'), and I felt super-super-uncomfortable. Don't end up caving and drinking because of the pressure. This is no way to party and if this happens, firmly and very seriously say, 'I would never force you to do something you weren't comfortable with, so don't do it to me.' Your serious tone will snap them out of the silliness and whilst they might seem off for a second (they will no doubt be a touch embarrassed), within no time it will be back to normal and you will be so proud of standing up for yourself and saying 'no'. Some of the best parties I've been to are the ones when I didn't have any alcohol – trust me, drinking is not nearly as glamorous as it looks!

GETTING HOME

I used to struggle a lot with getting home. I grew up in the far-out suburbs and then I moved to the countryside, and my dad liked to remind me that he wasn't a taxi and so wouldn't be collecting me at 'goodness knows what time'. Thank you, Dad. Always so supportive, haha! A good little trick is to stash away a £10 or £20 somewhere other than your purse. That way, if you lose your bag (please do try not to, though!) or make bad choices and spend all your money, you still have a little reserved for a cab home. I have been known to unabashedly pop a folded £20 note into my bra before we head out the door. I feel mighty smug come 1am when I know I can afford to get home easily.

Never, ever climb into an unlicensed minicab and always keep in touch with friends and let them know you'll call them as soon as you're home. Most times (even now) when I jump into a cab, I call home or a friend and say, 'Yes, I'm in the cab now, I took a picture of the licence plate and will be home in fifteen minutes.' That way, if the taxi driver had any intent of funny business, you've deterred him. I realise it's a bit mean of me to suspect everyone like this, but after several unpleasant accounts from friends, I've decided it's better to be safe than sorry!

BOYS. BOYS. BOYS

Now, the trickiest hurdle of any teen party is boys (or, if you're into them, girls). Since I'm into the men types, it's probably best if I talk about and give some advice on them (but we're all about loving everybody round here)!

For most of my time at school I attended an all-girls school, so boys were somewhat of a mystery to me. I never really understood what they expected from me and could never work out what I should do to 'be cool'. If I could go back to my teenage self and have a chat about this, I'd say, 'Louise, boys are like spiders, they're just as scared of you as you are of them.' Don't be afraid to offer a friendly hello and ask a question, or even to make an observation to get the conversation rolling. The most attractive thing you can be is confident (but not cocky) and the prettiest thing you can wear is a smile. There is absolutely nothing you can do to 'be cool' except not to try to be. Enjoy yourself, enjoy the party, fret less and everything will fall into place. Luckily for me, I now have Tiyana and Hollie, my two teenage sisters, whom I can impart this wisdom to.

Even as an adult, I still hold the same excitable place in my heart for a good party and that all begins when the invitation falls gently onto my doormat, pops into my inbox or pings on my phone.

19

First things first, when you see that lovely invite, check your diary to ensure you are free that day/ night. If you are, respond promptly – it can be quite embarrassing for you and the host if they have to chase you for a reply. Take a moment to consider whether there is any preparation you need to do for that event (new outfit, buy a gift, plan a babysitter, etc.) and plan that into your schedule too. By keeping on top of your event and party admin, you can sit back and relax.

WORK DOS

As I mentioned earlier, I've found that through my job I am invited to a lot of parties and I have learnt that there is a rather specific way of dealing with work dos, whether they are team-building evenings, mixers, launches or networking nights.

The most tippy top, super-duper and crucially important thing to remember at a work do is that, no matter how it is dressed up, it is still just that – a work do. It might well be the most glamorous, lavish, exciting event you have ever been to (I've been to some crazy amazing things) but if certain people are there (your boss, important clients, special customers, etc.), behave accordingly.

Often at these parties there's a free bar and complimentary nibbles, but this does not mean you need to go gaga. Naturally, it's good to relax a little, enjoy yourself, laugh and socialise, but you really don't want to be that girl who thinks she can booty drop at the Warner Brothers Christmas Dinner Party of 2013, just because she's finished off her rosé wine and that of her non-drinking friend's (thank you, Zoe). It's not a good look. It's especially not a good look when your friends are the UK's most popular vloggers and have cameras to hand – *cringe*.

I realise I sound somewhat of a goody two shoes but all I'm saying is don't make an utter fool of yourself, because I have and I didn't like it. At the time it was oh so hilarious, but looking back I just looked a bit silly. Don't make the same mistake I did!

👑 **A more positive tip for work parties** is to use it as an opportunity to strengthen bonds with your colleagues. Chances are there are people in your office/shop/zoo (if you are someone that works in a zoo, tweet me, it looks amazing!) that you rarely chat to or barely know. Use the social event as a chance to speak to them and find out more. I did this once and made one of my very best chummies, Emma. The wise and wonderful Oprah Winfrey once said, 'Every outing is an opportunity.' I tell myself that often and it puts me in such a good mind set.

Go to these kinds of events with an open mind, glad heart and responsible attitude, and you're going to have the very best time, I promise.

DINNER PARTIES

Another type of soirée I find myself attending more and more nowadays is dinner parties. In case you are unfamiliar, dinner parties are usually held in the host's home, a dinner is cooked, served, eaten, guests chat and eat and drink, and then it's through to the lounge for drinks, little nibbles, more chats and maybe a game or two. Sounds very dull but trust me, once you hit a certain age, it's basically the only way you want to spend a Friday night.

A couple of etiquette guildelines for this kind of evening include:

Politely warn the host/hostess if you have any specific food requirements, like not eating certain things on religious grounds, ethical grounds or because of allergies.

Ask if there's anything you can bring. More often than not your offer will be declined, but it's good manners to ask if you can make a side/dessert or provide any games.

Bring the host/hostess a gift. The standard is a bottle of bubbly but we like to add on a box of after dinner mints or a bunch of flowers too, just to say thank you for their efforts and hospitality.

If you have children, be clear on whether they are invited or whether it's an adults-only evening. If it's the latter, book your babysitter in good time. With two teenage sisters to hand, this is easy-peasy for me – yay!

Every now and again, the party baton is handed over and it's your turn to host the party. Wowee wowee wowee, the fun starts here. If, like me, you love to micro-manage every detail of an event, this is your time to shine, baaaabbbyy!

I start off by handwriting a guest list (oohh, I do love a good pen and notebook, which if you watch my videos, you well know). You may also need to decide on a theme, depending on what sort of event it is. If you are stuck for inspiration, as I mentioned earlier in the chapter, take yourself on a merry little jaunt on Pinterest and you'll be met with a wealth of ideas.

Personally, I prefer to host smaller soirées in my home rather than hire out a venue so I'll be focusing on that. If you, however, are a renting-places-out kinda guy or gal, don't be afraid to ask for extras (politely), be firm in your vision and be very clear about what you are getting for your money. It's better to be upfront from the very start, than in tears after (a lesson learnt the hard way, after my wedding venue made so many big mistakes on my special day – grrr).

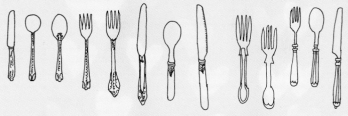

Before my guests arrive I have a big tidy-up and consider the impact extra people will have on my home. Do I need to make space for their shoes? (I know, how very boring of me, I do ask people to remove shoes – I have pale carpets!) Do I need to find a spot upstairs for coats? Have I got enough seats? Has one of the kitties left a present in their litter tray that needs a scoop and a scented candle lit? You know, the logical but not always obvious bits and pieces.

Once my lovelies are actually here, I am a fiend for constantly offering drinks (ensure you have a range of alcoholic and non-alcoholic ones to suit all tastes) and keeping people comfortable (I'll open windows, shut windows, fiddle with the heating, I get cray cray, haha).

 Top tip: If you're serving a lot of beverages is to pre-slice a few lemons and pop them in the freezer. That way, rather than offering 'ice and a slice', you can offer an iced slice! I tell this to absolutely everyone and always feel pleased with myself. Now this is in a published book, I'm just plain smug!

By the time I have relaxed into knowing everyone's thirst is well quenched, and that they're happy and enjoying themselves, I try and make time to talk to each of them and make every individual feel a little bit special. It's also good manners to thank everyone for coming, especially if they have travelled a long way or booked a hotel.

I think that the most important thing you can do as the host is to enjoy yourself too. When guests see you are relaxed and having a good time, they instantly relax a little bit more and the party is just a hit.

Parties are such a wonderful experience to have with other people. I would go as far as to say that if I could host or attend a party every single day, no matter what the type or theme, I would.

Next time you are at one, think positive thoughts, wear a smile, move with confidence, be friendly to people around you and have the absolute very, very, very best time. Also, let me know how it goes!

THINK **POSITIVE** THOUGHTS,

WEAR A **SMILE**,

MOVE WITH **CONFIDENCE**,

BE **FRIENDLY** TO PEOPLE
AROUND YOU

AND HAVE THE ABSOLUTE
VERY, VERY, VERY **BEST TIME**.

MEETING CELEBRITIES

Over the course of my life (but mostly with my job), I've come to meet a fair few celebrities. I've walked red carpets with them, I've talked at events with them, I've interviewed them, partied with them and filmed YouTube videos with them. That's a lot of interaction. You'd think I'd get over being star-struck but you'd be oh so wrong...

I am inherently awkward at social events and inevitably always mess things up. Somehow, I just always find a way. I'm talking confessing love to Lance Bass, nearly knocking over Steven Gerard's wife, hysterically crying all over Kylie and meeting Jamie Oliver at a flash party, when crawling out from a table on my hands and knees. (I did manage to get Kim Kardashian onside by helping her with her mobile phone, but that's another story!)

I think my meeting with KYLIE MINOGUE is one of my greatest (and for me, most embarrassing) tales. It was a roller coaster of cringe and toe-curling awkwardness but, now, looking back it makes me laugh.

It all started when I was chosen as one of the lucky few to make a short promotional video with Kylie at the YouTube Creator Space at Google HQ. Some of us YouTubers were contacted by Kylie's team, who wanted to discuss filming content as a way to promote Kylie and her new album, and, essentially, just have a lot of fun and learn from each other. But we were strictly told we'd only have twenty minutes to wrap the whole thing up. No extra time, no do-overs, just get it done. Already I felt pressured.

The event began with a Q&A, and we were seated on giant grey couches, with Kylie sat in front of us on a wooden chair. (Think primary school but you're older and your teacher is an international pop star!) Somewhat surreal.

It started OK. We went around the group introducing ourselves and giving a brief overview of our channels: 'Hi, I'm Louise. I make weekly videos about positive body image, beauty products, dressing to suit your figure and light entertainment.' Kylie nodded graciously. She was such a beauty, looking incredible in over-the-knee leather boots, jeans and a leather jacket.

So it was all going so well. Until she looked at me and very sweetly asked, 'When did you start here?' The panic. I just froze. This was not a hard question, but all of a sudden all I could do was look at Kylie Minogue and think, I remember when you got married on *Neighbours*. Your hair looked so fierce. I tried desperately to focus but it was like my brain was deliberately trying to ruin my chances of being cool. There was a pause. She blinked, I blinked, someone coughed, I said, 'Ummm do you mean here in this building or on YouTube?' She laughed. Nobody clarified. She carried on looking at me, this time with a caring smile and a slight lean forward. I had to answer... 'About 8.30am for the building, but about five years ago for YouTube,' I said. Covered both bases. What a win! I'd survived the Q&A. Kind of.

After a few more minutes of chit chat, Kylie was ushered away, group photos were taken and it was filming time. By this point, my stress levels were about six out of ten. I couldn't shake the intense you-have-twenty-minutes-onnnnllllyyyy feeling. What if I messed up? What if she hated the video concept? The idea of the video was that Kylie and I would each have half of my friend Jack's face to make up with any look we fancied that we thought represented Kylie's music. What if I wasn't funny or sparkly or engaging? But wait, I couldn't let myself be dragged down by my insecurities. You are a successful, smart, beautiful woman, I told myself. You've got this in the bag. My friend Jack and I were sat waiting on the pre-lit set, whilst cameramen,

management, journalists and my friend Hazel (who was also feeling rather dithery) stood looking on.

In walked Kylie. It. Was. Tense.

Stress levels increased to seven now.

This was a timed challenge, so once the klaxon rang, the adrenaline kicked in and a frantic scrabbling for make-up brushes began. Jack was being completely charming, Kylie was working her artistic magic and I, well, I was coming unstuck. I tried so desperately to hold it together but I think the number of people in the room, my extreme lack of any artistic ability and the fact that I was sat inches away from such a renowned performer – it all just hit me. Stress levels at a nine, I began to crumble. It started off small with me making a mess of Jack's face, but then I started full-naming everyone: 'Oh I love the shading you're doing there Kylie Minogue!', 'How does that feel on your face Jack Howard?' As we wrapped up the video, Kylie said, 'Okay!' and (clearly after my brain had shut down) I randomly yelled: 'I've got an auntie called Kaye!'

Silence.

Good job, Louise.

With my official twenty minutes over and after lots of 'thank you's and 'such a pleasure's, Kylie was gone, and I was left thinking about the mess I had made of the video. I felt like I could've done better; I could have been wittier, or sharper, or more vibrant – but I wasn't. I just left the funnies to Jack and kind of coasted through. Sensing my sadness, Jack asked what was wrong and I began to cry.

At first it was one of those beautiful pearly white tears, but then more came. More, and more, and more until I had worked myself up into a full sob, complete with dry heaving and periodic shivers. I was a mess. Lucky for me, I was on an empty set. Until Kylie walked back in. She'd forgotten something and, in popping back for it, discovered a hunched-over, blubbering woman who looked like a warthog that had just run a marathon in the desert. Kylie spotted me and came straight over to see what was wrong. This is the moment where I could have (and maybe should have) lied. I could've said I'd had some bad news or extreme hay fever, but instead I sniffled away, telling her I thought I did a bad job as she calmly, whilst holding my hand and stroking my knee, told me it was fine. Looking back, I suppose it was. And after a good old cry we both just laughed about it and I saw the funny side of things.

☆ ☆ ☆

Something that helps when I'm faced with these rather glitzy situations is remembering that celebrities are only really celebrities because you or I made them that way. They aren't celebrities to their grans! They (well, most of them) wouldn't introduce themselves as a famous person. They are the same as everyone else, they just happen to have very well-known skills, talents or positions.

Sometimes, when people who watch my videos meet me, they fluster and panic, and I always remind them that we're standing on the same level and are exactly the same. Celebrities want what you want – to be talked to nicely and to have a pleasant experience with you.

Take it from someone who has both screamed at people on stages (oh me, oh my! I love a concert!) and has been screamed at on stages, from someone who has cried in front of pop stars, fluffed words in front of 'It Girls' and popped up from under tables next to famous chefs, it's alright in the end. If they are decent people, they will see the funny side of it and laugh along.

Next time you rub shoulders with the glitterati, STAY CALM AND BE FRIENDLY – remember you are just as worthy as they are. Humans are humans, after all.

The Art of Shopping

It wasn't until I was a teenager that I found my joy in shopping. For the best part of my childhood, I'd thought shopping was a chore to be endured, rather than the pleasurable experience I find it now. I'm going to explore the ways you can make shopping more of a treat and ways you can squeeze the very most out of those precious hours.

Before we discuss all my tips and tricks, we should familiarise ourselves with the common shopping pitfalls that so many of us fall victim to.

Self-confidence The biggest one that I personally find myself coming unstuck at is self-confidence. I think we've all been there. I think we've all been in that place where you pick up a couple of clothing items to try on, schlep off to the fitting rooms, undress in the badly lit, tiny cubicles, put on the dress/jeans/top and feel... well, disgusting. I don't quite know what it is that makes changing rooms just about the worst place to feel great, but there is something. It might be the combination of stark fluorescent lighting and the fact you're wearing that cocktail dress with your socks, standing on tippy toes to imagine your legs in heels. But essentially, I always feel a little bit crummy in those places. We're going to talk about ways to beat this!

Money Another of my downfalls used to be mismanaging my money. A long time ago, when I was at university, we had a Christmas party to go to ('The Snow Ball' to be precise. See what they did there? See?) and naturally, 19-year-old Louise wanted to wow the crowds in something pale and iridescent, as was fashionable in the early Noughties. I headed off to Debenhams with my Auntie Judith and spent what felt like hours trying on various ball gowns. Eventually, after Auntie Ju having a little cry in the fitting rooms about how beautiful she thought I looked (literally the best response to dress trying-on ever), I waltzed up to the till to pay. On handing over my card and swiping it through the machine, I discovered it had been declined and a red-faced trip to the cash point straight after showed that, actually, I didn't have nearly as much money as I had anticipated. Moral of the story here is to check your bank balance before you go somewhere and avoid stuttering embarrassedly to the shop assistant about how you'll come back later with cash. As it happens, I never did get that A-line, champagne-coloured dress and ended up going to the ball in my Sixth Form end-of-year party dress and having a great time. Phew!

Expectations Two other very little things that I often find have a bit of a negative impact are going shopping with the wrong people (I'm talking about the ones that rush you or tut disapprovingly when you pick up something you like or only let you go in the shops THEY like), or running in with the wrong expectations. There have been far too many times when on the drive into town I have imagined a beautiful creation that not only will be everything I want it to look like, but make me look two sizes slimmer, be half-price in a sale and be the thing that every person ever compliments me on. It doesn't exist. I fabricated it in my head. Now I'm just in the maze that is Topshop, feeling sad that I haven't designed my own clothing range and wishing I could magic something up. Don't do this. Let's spend some time later talking about realistic shopping goals.

So we've addressed some of the perils of shopping, let's now focus on the areas we can excel in to make trips to the shops a pleasure.

Time

In my humble opinion (which really is all this book is about, my humble opinions), the quickest way to success is timing. There are two elements to timing actually. Firstly, allow yourself plennntttyyy of time. Allow yourself the time to get to and from the shops in a leisurely fashion. Allow yourself time to wander around, browse the aisles and idly feel the fabrics. Allow yourself time to try clothes on, to stop for comfort breaks and to pause for snacks, lunch or dinner. Make shopping an event. Put it in your diary and respect it as its own activity. By doing this you are instantly lowering your stress levels and allowing space for enjoyment and satisfaction.

When to shop

The second timing element is choosing precisely when to shop. If it's supermarket shopping, I would suggest first thing in the morning or very late at night (a lot of larger stores are open twenty-four hours a day now). This means that if you are frustrated by manoeuvring your trolley around 600 others you can avoid it and, if you shop in the evening, a lot of produce is usually marked down so you can find some brilliant bargains. If you are heading out for clothes shopping, force yourself out of bed early and enjoy shopping just as the store opens. That way it won't be very busy, the clothes will all be hung beautifully and in size order (we've all seen those shops at 4.30pm on a Saturday, where it looks like the Apocalypse has struck) and you can try things on in peace.

These two tips alone will stand you in good stead and be a huge leap towards mastering the art of shopping.

Eat

You know those people who find themselves angry when they're hungry? That's me. I call it hangry. If I'm not fed and watered, my fuse is shorter, my emotions higher and my all-round stress levels are soaring. I'm fairly sure this isn't a rare quality and that everyone functions better when they have had a lovely brunch (eggs Benedict and an orange juice please) and when they're not thinking about dehydration headaches and rumbly tummies.

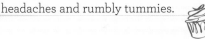

ON YOUR SHOPPING EXCURSIONS, MAKE SURE TO SCHEDULE IN YUMMY STOPS TO REFUEL AND FEEL HAPPY.

If you are shopping with littles

Fill your bag with snacks and treats for their tiny tummies. Avoid super-sugary items that make energy levels spike, unless you are also adding in time for them to be unstrapped from pushchairs and allowed to run wild. Some shopping centres actually have playground or activity spaces for these kinds of things (clever), so it might be worth checking. Natural sugar snacks like fruit or unsalted crackers are always a winner in my books. Sometimes, though, if I'm feeling brave (or just plain crazy), I'll pick up one of those marshmallow sprinkle pops from Starbucks and let Baby Glitter enjoy that whilst I um and ahh over that sequinned kimono top that I know I'll never have the balls to wear. Do this at your own peril though – the mess and hyperactivity that spring from such treats are spectacular!

Preparation

A practical point worth remembering if you are shopping for clothes, shoes, bags or anything that you actually put on is to spend a little bit of preparation time the night before or earlier in the day, making yourself feel your best. By that, I mean taking time in the shower to shave your legs, or putting a little bit of make-up on, or moisturising your arms, or painting your nails. I have found that if I feel pretty and lovely whilst I am choosing new things for myself, it is easier to imagine them on and easier to like what I see in the mirror.

Love your body

As I said earlier, self-confidence can make or break a shopping day. I have had many a trip where I ended up putting everything back on the rail and was left feeling deflated and altogether downbeat about myself. I think we've all been there. Now, before I go for trips where I know I'll be in changing rooms or I'll be selecting things for myself, I do take the time to feel physically lovely, but I also remind myself that I am fine as I am. It's quite alright to love the shape you are, to accept that some things are not going to work for your figure (pencil skirts and crop tops, I'm looking at you) and to embrace the things that do (hello skater skirts and nipped in dresses). We are all our own worst critics. The clothes don't tell us we aren't good enough, we do. We need to learn to love the body we have, cherish the parts we love, adorn it with beautiful things we like and enjoy the process of shopping for and finding those things.

The next time you are in a shop or a fitting room and feeling down about yourself, remember that there's no grand jury on the definition of a beautiful body. You get to decide.

Decide you are gorgeous and you are.

If, after spending some time taking care of your body and mind, you still can't drag yourself out of that thought bog, then leave it. There will be other days for shopping and if you completely force yourself and have a terrible, awful time, the experience will have an impact on your overall outlook on shopping and make you hate it. Every now and again, it's ok to throw in the towel and give up – you can always try again another day.

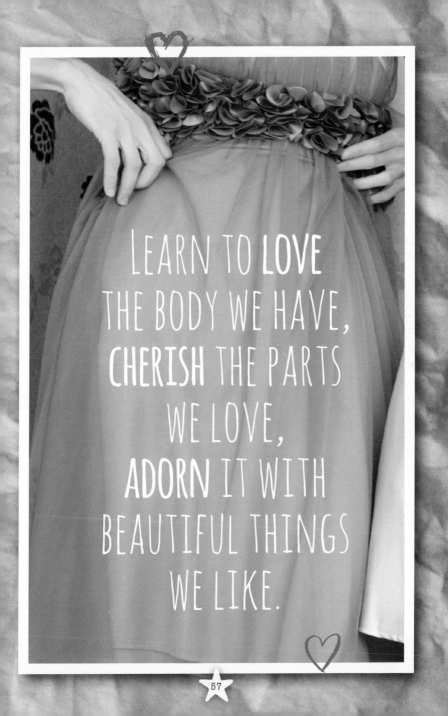

LEARN TO **LOVE** THE BODY WE HAVE, **CHERISH** THE PARTS WE LOVE, **ADORN** IT WITH BEAUTIFUL THINGS WE LIKE.

57

Shopping buddies

Something I find that really helps with feeling good on the inside is taking the right people with you. For example, my dad is a lovely chap but often finds himself making comments about my weight and so, in turn, I feel a bit low. He would be an absolute no-no to shop with. My friend Zoe, however, points out my beautiful parts and helps find outfits or items that flatter, and so I feel lifted by her presence.

Pick people who find the joy in you and you're going to have a good time. Not only that, if you shop with people whose taste or style you admire, you have a handy second opinion and an extra set of eyes to scout for hidden gems on the rails. If it's totally unavoidable for you to shop with someone who perhaps isn't ideal (you might be a little younger and still having to shop with parents or relatives, etc.), then ask if you can go to certain areas of the shop by yourself so that you can have calm, non-judgemental moments whilst you look at what's available. Maybe suggest your mum checks out the dresses whilst you have a quick look-see at the casuals. There is never a need to be rude or hurt their feelings, just be tactful and gentle and things will turn out well.

What to wear and take

Practical time again! If you know you're likely to be out for a good few hours, think about what you're wearing. Those skinny jeans and strappy heels might look divine, but are you still going to feel fancy and fabulous three hours in? No. You are not. You are going to hate every step and wish you weren't so restricted. Opt for easy breezy clothing that is comfortable – something that won't make you detest life after hours of wear and, if you are planning on visiting fitting rooms, choose something you can whip on and off easily. There have been times when I haven't taken this advice and it's ruined the entire day. That zip-up dress that I couldn't undo myself was a rookie mistake, I tell you. Also, use your smarts and consider what might be helpful to chuck in your handbag before you leave the house. Lip balm, mints or chewing gum and my emergency (shhhh, shopping can be vital) credit card are all on my list.

SALES

Now, we've talked about arriving early to beat the regular shoppers, but we need to have a chat about arriving early for sales. Sales are a whole different ball game. Sales are like the Olympic games of shopping.

People. Love. Sales.

First things first, think hard. Do you reeaaallyy care about this sale? Is it chock-a-block full of items you have been lusting over for months, or is it just because that very standard pair of jeans are £15, down from £45? Do you actually love the jeans? I say all this because I have fallen prey to the madness of a sale before. About six years ago, my friend Nicki and I decided to go to the winter Next sale with her then 2-year-old daughter, Sophie. We got up and dressed and trekked out in the cold at about 5am (seriously, 5AM), and headed over to the retail park. On arrival, it was clear that every woman in Northampton had had the same idea and was queuing up, ready. We queued, women ran, Nicki darted like an athlete to the children's section, whilst I cowered over by the catalogue stand with Sophie, hoping I wouldn't be knocked over. All thoughts of flicking through rails of reduced-priced clothing were immediately abandoned as hordes of women threw every scrap of fabric they could find into giant clear bin bags and scurried over to the tills. It wasn't fun. It was chaotic and frustrating and hot and, in my opinion, not worth it. I would actually prefer to pay a little bit more and enjoy the experience.

That said, if you have truly thought about it and you do have your heart set on something, throw yourself into the arena and grab away! It might be worth your while doing a little research before you don your flats and easy-on-easy-off attire.

Research

Whether you're searching the sales or window shopping after a day at work/home/school, take a little bit of time to research. If you have found some bits and bobs you love, check online to see if there are any printable vouchers you could use or Google whether that store will be having a sale very soon. Also, take this research as an opportunity to see if any other shops are stocking the same thing but at a more affordable price. This can be applied quite well to beauty products because a lot of stores stock the same brands but have different offers at different times. In terms of clothing or shoes, if you have used the product before, know what sizes will definitely fit you. Also, always consider shopping online and feel smug that you scored a bargain without ever leaving your sofa!

If your heart is set on having a great, big shopping spree day (let's face it, they're kind of the best), then just take a couple of moments to research deals and offers, have a look at parking and routes (once we decided to shop in Birmingham, did no research and wasted an hour in traffic and then looking for parking space – learn from my mistake here), and also have a rough idea of where suitable lunch restaurants or cafes are.

If you are shopping with toddlers or babies, a good idea would be to figure out where the nicest or nearest change facilities are. When Darcy was a teeny-tiny, I used to love using John Lewis's facilities because they were always clean, well-stocked and there was a cosy little private area for mamas who didn't feel like feeding in public.

That lil' bit of planning will go a long, long way to making your day fabulous.

Lists

⭐ Now that you have your discounts or deals planned, your parking spot sorted and best friend to hand, it might be wise to make a list. Spend a brief moment thinking about what it is you need or what it is you think you might fancy. Sometimes, if I go shopping without any ideas, I wander endlessly and have no focus. You don't need to be crazy clear of every single item you'll be coming home with, but something along the lines of: birthday gift for best friend, keep eyes peeled for sparkly shoes or gold bag, basic tees to replace tatty old ones and that new amazing book *Life with a Sprinkle of Glitter* (heh heh).

⭐ Alternatively, it's sometimes fun to make a list by event. So for example, if I know I have a lot coming up in the next few weeks, I'll write a list of the things I have to go to and then I know that I need an outfit, accessory, gift or travel item for it. Smart huh?

⭐ By having a loose guide to what you need or want, you are closer to ensuring a successful shopping trip and making sure you don't forget anything.

Remember
- Preparation
- Time
- Money
- Self-confidence
- Positive attitude

Try something new

One of the biggest things that changed my perception of shopping, from it being a bore to it being a fun way to spend time, was trying new things. The beauty of most shops is that you can give things a little whirl before you part with your hard-earned pennies. If you are at a make-up stand, sample the product, or if it is a high-end counter, ask the assistant to apply some of the make-up to your face and see if you like it. You could really be adventurous and try something you would never normally go for and the absolute worst-case scenario is that you need to wipe it off. If it is particularly out of your comfort zone, have the assistant apply it, walk around the shopping centre for a few hours to allow yourself to become accustomed to the new shade and then go back and purchase it if you feel willing. Never be pressured into completing a transaction (remember, a lot of sales people work on commission so it is in their best interests if you buy lots of lovely things) and never be afraid to tell someone you'd like to think about it.

Unfortunately, with clothes you can't really walk round the entire shopping precinct in the outfit before purchasing (without getting into some serious trouble!), but of course they do have changing rooms. Take this opportunity to try styles you'd never think would suit you or put on colours you have previously shied away from. If they really look vile, just hang them back up and relax, knowing that at least you tried!

👑 A little tip though, try taking a few things in at once – try some outfits that are out of your comfort zone and some that you feel quite confident will look nice. It can be a bit depressing to take in a heap of clothes and look rubbish in all of them, so having that 'safe piece' amongst your stash will cheer you up and help you fight the blues!

Have a postive attitude

Whether you are shopping for clothes, beauty, food, electronics or something entirely different and whether you're online, in a shopping centre or hunting for treasure in boutiques and charity shops, the absolute best tip I can give you is to go in to it with a positive attitude. Shopping is a privilege; it's something to be enjoyed and a luxury to be grateful for. It's something you can share with friends, laugh and relax during and feel proud of (after you've showcased your bargain hunting skills!). And you'll feel happy and excited to take home your shiny fresh bags of sparkly new things.

I hope all my tips will help you master the art of shopping and that you find some beautiful treasures next time you head off on your spree!

Travelling in Style

Travelling is a thing we all do to some degree, and it's something we can all make the most of and enjoy if we have the right attitude, and if we're prepared for it. In this chapter, we are going to explore all of the ways we can make travelling a super-easy and fun experience for ourselves because, hey, if you're gonna travel, you may as well do it in style, right?

Since my YouTube channels and my blog became my full-time gig, I have found travelling has become part and parcel of normal life for me. I travel on the train to London a few times a week, whilst I'm there I'm jumping on and off tubes and in and out of taxis, or finding my way (usually very clumsily) on foot. I also fly out to conventions or shows a lot, so this involves plenty of time in airports, on airplanes and in hotels. On top of that, I do all the usual pootling about on errands and doing mum stuff, in a car or with the buggy. Essentially, I'm always on the move and I feel confident in saying I'm getting pretty darn good at it.

this space for correspondence

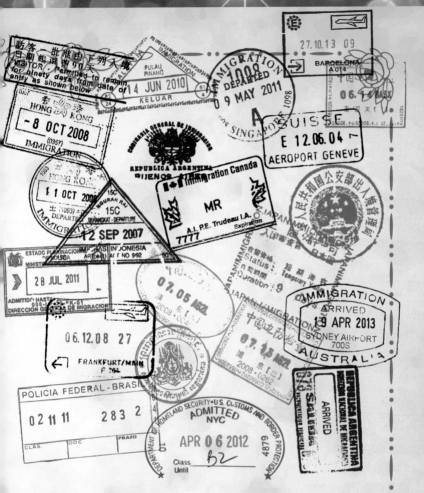

The key to travelling well is preparation. Plan for any issues that could arise, so that when they do, you've got it under control. You are a calm, confident woman (or gentleman, of course) who is in total control. You have a place to get to, you're gonna get there and you're going to look fabulous doing it. Let's talk about how!

this space for address only

Walking

Whether you're walking 3 miles to school in the freezing sleet/ boiling sunshine (thanks Dad, you're right, it was 'character building', but I'm still bitter about it) or jumping from the nearest tube stop to the office, be prepared for the 'on foot' parts of your journey. I have too many times fallen at the 'these flats are so cute and comfy, I'll wear them to work this morning... ARRRGGHHHH the pavement is the slightest bit damp and now my shoes are soaked and I need an industrial strength hairdryer to dry them otherwise I'm going to get gout' hurdle. We've all been there. It's awful. Or what about that day you thought it looked chilly, donned your feet with (let's face it, mock) UGGS and then it turned out to be the warmest day in October since records began, and you were so over-heated you wanted to rip off your furry foot-ovens and throw them into on coming traffic? OK, perhaps a bit strong there, but you see where I'm going with this. These issues can be avoided.

The night before you take your big steps into the great outdoors, have a sneaky look at the weather and plan accordingly. Apply your findings to footwear, jackets and umbrellas/sunglasses too. You'll thank yourself for it and feel slightly smug when your sandal-clad feet strut past all those silly UGG wearers!

Something else to consider whilst you're trotting (comfortably, in the appropriate attire) from A to B is that you have a unique opportunity that those in planes, trains and automobiles don't have: you can stop. It's such a tiny thing, but I couldn't not share it – use this time wisely. As you are dashing from place to place, look around you. Are you taking a shortcut through a lovely park? Is there a cute little bakery/shop/market on your way? Does the sun look pretty twinkling through the leaves above? These are the things I look for and then snap on my phone. Then, when I'm at my desk or have a lull, I flick through my saved pictures and choose a few to throw onto social media – I think Instagram is my favourite. You might apply this to other things. My sister is an art student in London and she takes snaps on the go of things she is inspired to paint. I have another friend who once made a whole blog out of the beautiful things she saw as she was walking places. All the beauty is there if you have an open attitude to finding it. It's in those tiny, little things that I find happiness.

Catching Trains

I have an American friend who recently told me she has never, ever been on a train. Apparently, unless you live in the kind of city to have a subway, this is pretty commonplace in the US. In England, on the other hand, trains are a very regular part of life and something I spend an awful lot of time on. At first, I would just while away my time listening to music or watching the world outside the window whizz by, but now I'm a seasoned traveller, I've found better things to do.

The trick to making train time work for you is to be efficient. It's already kinda frustrating that you have to take so much time out of the day to be sat on a train, so you may as well try to get things done whilst you're on one. Once, and this may be taking it too far, I sat next to a man who pulled a china bowl, metal spoon, little ziplock bag of cereal and bottle of milk out of his briefcase. No joke. He sat and calmly ate the cereal, put the bowl and spoon in the empty ziplock bag and placed it back in the case. Seriously. I mean, that's one way to be efficient with time in the mornings, but let's look at some other ideas too!

My go-to activity for trains is editing. For my YouTube channels, I film and edit a lot of videos. Since editing requires no internet (and as internet is a rarity on most trains), it's the ideal job to tackle in those minutes and hours you have spare. I always feel so accomplished when I complete a video whilst on the go – I feel like I've cheated time or something. Have a think about whether there is anything like that you could crack on with. Do you have an assignment or project you could work on? Trains are great places to focus without any interruptions. Also, the satisfaction you feel after you have ticked something off your list is enough to make any journey worth it.

👑 **Pro tip for travelling with electronics like laptops and tablets:** Look for handbags that accommodate those items. I'm not really a fan of the traditional laptop case (plus I worry that it just highlights the fact you are carrying something valuable to muggers – I worry about these things!), but last year I found an amazing black handbag in Zara that has a padded compartment for laptops, as well as a padded smaller section for iPads. It's genius! It looks just like a suave day bag, but hidden inside you are a high-powered go-getter!

If working is something you don't want to fill your travelling time with (and really, I don't blame you), why not use this time to catch up on other bits and pieces. I find travelling on trains the perfect time to reply to all those texts I've been meaning to respond to, as well as scrolling through Twitter, Tumblr and Instagram. You'll have all the warm fuzzies after a few chitchats with some of your nearest and dearest, plus you won't lose points for not replying. Win.

If all else fails, use this time to enjoy something low tech. Flick through your favourite magazine, finish off your make-up if you were in a rush when you left the house, or spend twenty minutes catching some precious zzzs.

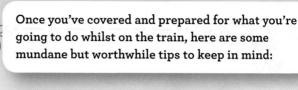

Once you've covered and prepared for what you're going to do whilst on the train, here are some mundane but worthwhile tips to keep in mind:

↪ **If you can, book online.** You will often find much more affordable tickets and deals this way. You can also reserve seats and on some trains choose to be at tables or closer to amenities (like the café carriage, the tinklywinkly department or precious, precious plug sockets).

◎ **Some train lines have an electric socket** for every set of seats, but others (including the line I use) don't. A wonderful girl (who chatted to me because she watched my videos – yay YouTube) once let me in on a secret. At the end of every London Midland carriage, behind the seat, is a socket. I can't tell you how many times this has come in handy on the 11.55pm train when I've had 3 per cent phone battery left. Thank you girl of secrets for sharing this!

⫸ **A lot of trains have a trolley service** that you can buy refreshments from but just like the sockets, some don't. Be prepared and carry water and snacks with you in case of delays. This one is especially prudent if you're travelling with children.

🐚 **When the train pulls into the platform, do not rush.** Every single person on that moving tin can is going to stand up, fluster, grab bags and rush off as soon as possible. Then, at busy stations, there is going to be a bottleneck and a fair bit of standing about at the ticket barriers. Be savvy, take your time, put your jacket on and saunter off the train once everyone has done all their rushing. Then you'll be the cool, calm, together person who glides through the gates in style.

Planes

Travelling by plane is undoubtedly the most stylish way to travel and, for me, the most exciting. Whether it's a holiday or a business trip, I plan, plan, plan that plane ride because I want to enjoy it as much as I possibly can! This year I have flown numerous times, sometimes on quick European flights, sometimes transatlantic, sometimes alone, sometimes with friends and sometimes with my 3-year-old daughter. All types of journey have their different challenges, but all of them can totally be styled out.

Top tip: If you can, leave yourself plenty of time and you'll be winning at this. Give yourself ample time at home to plan what you want to take in your hand luggage and allow plenty of time for airport browsing.

Hand luggage is the bag you are allowed to take inside the actual cabin with you and is your key to a great flight. I have an allocated bag that I bought about a year ago in the Accessorize sale, which I use purely for flights (and then for day trips whilst I'm away – when I went to Seattle with my daughter, Darcy, it became the perfect toddler tote!). When you're looking for one, search under the 'weekender' category. You want that bag to be roomy enough for all your gubbins, but not so big that it exceeds the airline's size limits.

First things first with your hand luggage bag: have a separate compartment for your purse, phone, passport and travel documents. Always use the same compartment. Trust me. This way, when you need to whip out your passport for the fifty million checks they have, or you need your money for that last Chocolate

Cream Frappucino with a shot of peppermint (do it), it's to hand. You won't be scrambling around the bottom of your bag in a fluster and panic, you can just pop your hand in, pull your needed thing out and voilà – you are one smooth criminal. Although not actually a criminal, just a smart, suave traveller. #NoCrimePlease

Once you have the bag and the crucial compartment down, consider what else you'll need onboard. If it's a quickie flight, probably not much more than headphones and a book (hopefully this one, heh heh) or tablet, but for the sake of this chapter, let's pretend we're going on a long-haul flight.

When I pack hand luggage, I prepare for the worst. Imagine when you arrive at your destination, your suitcase does not arrive with you. You need to wait a day for it to be delivered to your hotel, so what do you do? Rush out and buy a ton of make-up and new clothes? No. You are a stylish traveller. You've already read this chapter and have prepared for this event. In your hand luggage, you have packed a spare outfit (including underwear), as well as a tiny bag of toiletries and make-up. You now have time to enjoy your first day and await your main bag. Phew!

When considering that 'emergency pack', go for an outfit that's lightweight and easy to fold. If I'm going somewhere warm, I just throw a little striped dress that I know I don't actually need to wear a bra with. I know it goes with any shoes and will work from beach to bar. I roll it up super tight (along with a fresh pair of knickers) and squeeze it into a small ziplock bag. It takes up hardly any space, but gives me so much peace of mind. Also, if something huge spilt on you during the flight (red wine in shaky hands of man next to me, I'm looking at you), you have a backup.

Make-up and toiletries are something I put a lot of consideration into as well. If I can, I just take my entire make-up bag with me onboard. I tend not to take huge amounts of cosmetics with me as I have my make-up routine down to a tee. I know that with a twelve-shade shadow palette I can create different looks, and I will take 2–3 lip shade options so that I can go from bare minimum to full glitz in no time at all. To save limited space, I decant a lot of liquid products (such as foundation, moisturiser, primer, etc.) into little plastic containers that you can buy from most supermarkets or pharmacies and I also have minis of many things (like cleansers, deodorants or dry shampoos). Remember to check your airline's policy before flying to see what quantities you can take onboard. For safety reasons, there is a limit on liquids.

I also make sure to always bring a travel toothbrush (the kind that you can fold into itself so the bristles remain clean), a mini tube of toothpaste, make-up wipes (remember 'flights, fannies and festivals'?) and some hair bobbles/kirby grips.

If I'm travelling with friends, I might pack something fun in my make-up bag, like face masks so that we can have a little pamper party. The best kind are the individually wrapped pre-soaked tissue types. They avoid all the messiness, are easy to apply (you simply position them on your face) and they're easy to clear up afterwards. Try it, it's a lot of fun and leaves you feeling pretty great too! A word to the wise though, as you're proudly sat like a soggy rag doll with a giant cloth on your face, you're gonna get some awkward looks from fellow passengers. Ignore and feel glad that your skin is having such a lovely time. You'll be glowing at the arrival gates!

Now that you have your essentials ticked off the list (passport, travel documents, money, backup clothes, toiletries), pack your electronics. I love to blog and vlog everything, so I tend to carry my laptop, my point 'n' shoot camera, my canon DSLR, my phone, headphones and, if I'm travelling with my little girl, a fully kid-friendly film- and app-loaded iPad. Oh, also, I have toddler-friendly headphones too – they are teeny and crazy cute. Something I want to add to my collection is a portable phone charger so that if my battery runs out, I don't need to scout out a socket at the airport, I'm all covered!

Now for the fun part – snacks and extras! Although long-haul flights will offer you an array of snacks and meals, I always like to have a few extra treats on board. Have a nosey through duty free and treat yourself to some of the tax-free chocolates!

As for extras, think about what applies to you. My friend Zoe feels the cold really easily (and planes can get nippy), so she always brings extra socks and a cosy sweater to keep herself snuggly. If you are travelling with littles, bring small toys, colouring books, puzzles and comfort blankets. Last year, I went to Florida with my two teenage sisters and one tweenage brother and made them surprise 'fun packs' (quizzes, sweets, challenges, etc.) for when boredom hit – a great way to begin any adventure.

Now that you have your bag packed and you've splurged in duty free (oh Origins skincare, why are you so gloriously tempting?), it's time to sit back and enjoy the flight. Remember to keep hydrated (that recycled air isn't the best) by drinking lots of water and moisturising your skin, be sure to move about and take regular walks to keep your circulation going and if you're not too excited, take a well-earned nap!

On arrival, to achieve that stylish celebrity-at-airport look, throw everything into your giant bag (don't have things hanging out or clutched in your hands, think chic), don your oversized sunglasses or drape your scarf round your shoulders and walk tall. You are a seasoned jet-setter after all!

We've spent a lot of time talking about how good preparation can be your absolute saviour, but sometimes it's just not an option. Sometimes, spontaneity wins out and you have to seize the day and go with the flow. Do not miss out on these times. They are the stuff of belly laughs and amazing memories. In these cases, when you don't have your phone charger or lip balm, prepare mentally. Remind yourself that someone will have those things and that everything will be fine. Stay calm and embrace the moment. Remember that it's perfectly alright to let yourself have an adventure, big or small, and that the most important thing to take with you is a positive attitude and a massive smile. Oh, and if you can, snap a few pictures – you'll want to remember all this in years to come!

Create

SETTING UP HOME 80

PRETTIFYING YOUR ROOM 92

CRAFTS 108

ANTI-BAKING 122

SETTING UP HOME

Whether you are moving into student halls, nesting in your city flat with a lovebird, or buying your 'forever house' in the suburbs, setting up home is a big, fun and sometimes daunting job. In this section, we'll explore some of the ways you can make setting up your home a bit easier, and things you can do to your current home to spruce it up a little and help things run smoother.

Before I moved to university, I had lived at home my entire life and never really worried about things like the price of cheese, a TV licence or how many sets of bedding I would need. Things seemed to magically happen, food appeared in the fridge, bedding was always fresh and the TV just TV'd. Lovely, lovely.

On taking the big plunge and applying to a few universities, it dawned on me that if I was accepted (thank you Liverpool for having me!), I would be flying the nest, moving on to pastures new and being an independent woman. Oh yeah! *Clicks fingers in sassy 'S' shape*

The day rolled around, and after a slightly surprising set of A level results, I was offered my place. We put the deposit down on my teeny tiny slither of a room in student halls and it was time to pack!

At the time, my home life was pretty topsy-turvy and so I had to make a lot of decisions myself. I learnt a lot of (sometimes expensive, sometimes frustrating) lessons along the way. So, lucky duckies, I'm going to impart that knowledge to you and hopefully save you a little bit of angst for when it's your big moment to step out into the world.

STUDENT DIGS

When moving out for the first time, pack sensibly. On hearing I'd been given a place, I immediately packed about twenty pairs of strappy heels, a hundred going-out dresses and a meagre three casual day-wear items. It didn't take me long to assess, unpack and repack, but don't let your excitement get the better of you. Think about where you are going to live and what the climate is like there. Pack a few dressy items for nights out and evening events but also, since you are there mainly to study, casual, comfy, easy clothes. Remember, the wardrobes in most student dwellings are not huge and so capsule wardrobes are key.

You're also going to need a full set of bedding, most likely including pillows and a duvet. In this department, 18-year-old Louise made one good choice and one silly choice. The good one was the duvet; I bought something that was actually two duvets attached together with small buttons. It meant that in the warmer months you could take the two apart, store one away and just use the one. This was great in the summer, when I only needed something light to cover me. In the winter, I just kept the pair connected, popped the duvet cover on and voilà! Snug as a bug in a rug (did anyone else's mum used to say that at bedtime or just mine?). The silly choice was with sheeting and duvet/pillow cases. For some reason, I splashed out a lot of my budget on very upmarket bedding that, whilst completely beautiful, was totally extravagant and not at all necessary for my single student bed. If I had been sensible I would have picked something from a supermarket or more affordable brand. Even though now I can afford to splurge a little on something more luxurious, I still pick up lovely bedding sets from Primark!

Once your wardrobe and bedding is tackled, you need to think about the bathroom. A lot of student places now have bathrooms en suite, but even if they do, it's still worth thinking about a compact, but well-supplied, cleaning kit. With lots of people sharing the facilities, it is essential to be on top of everything and keep everywhere fresh. Obviously, it's entirely up to you what you have but I would definitely advise rubber gloves, a couple of cloths and sponges, a bottle of bleach, antibacterial spray and some glass cleaner (think shower doors and mirrors). We had a running joke at university that if I was deep-cleaning my en suite, I must have an assignment due in – I would find any excuse to do something else before sitting down to write essays. Haha!

THE GAL-PAL PALACE

By the time I was in second year and moving in to an apartment with four **good friends**, we had the living situation down to an art and things ran a lot smoother. But it was time to wave goodbye to the city-centre student halls and say hello to a rather grotty house, on an equally grotty estate. Inside the house however, there was not a spot of grot to be found. My four girlfriends and I transformed that five-bedroom terrace into a palace of **scatter cushions**, sweet curtains and cosy nooks. It took a bit of work, but we set that home up beautifully and made it our own.

The first thing we tackled when our little hands had hold of the keys was general **cleanliness**. We held off on moving our belongings in so that we could clean the entire house, top to bottom. Cleaning is a lot easier when you aren't working around things and you can work through much more quickly. With five of us and our boyfriends, it only took a day or two to completely **blitz** it and then we were able to crack on with the next task: decorating.

We each had our own bedroom, so this wasn't too hard to deal with. Select your colour (I obviously went for the loudest shade of pink I could find), **paint paint paint**, leave to dry, done! A little tip for painting – run a line of masking tape along the crease between the top of the wall and your ceiling as well as along the skirting board. This will (hopefully) prevent you from making a lot of messy paint splodges and strokes where you don't want them! Also, it's worth laying down a dust sheet on your floor (you can pick up very cheap plastic ones of these in most DIY or decorating stores) – it will stop you from ruining the carpets, especially if you have pernickety landlords!

We had **house meetings** to decide what we wanted to do about shared spaces and decided on white paint for bathrooms, large, cream, dusky pink and sage throws for the horrid patterned sofas, and a butter-cream yellow for the walls in our garden. I say 'garden', but what I actually mean is an 8ft by 8ft concrete yard, attached to the back door. We know it's this big because one summer we thought it would be easy to squeeze an 8ft by 6ft **inflatable pool** out there, and it wasn't. At all. We managed to arrange it so that you quite literally stepped out of the back door and into it. Very practical!

For the girls who didn't like their curtains, we looked around good-value high-street shops like Wilkinsons. And for throws, cushions, lamps, rugs and other **soft touches** that really make such a difference, we all loaded into my friend Faye's car and jollied round IKEA. A word to the wise, IKEA is a maze of enchanting goodies and whilst you might be going in for only two big frames and a mirror, you're coming out with those, plus three scatter cushions, a small table, a storage system, a set of **fairy lights** and a pack of vanilla scented tea lights. I don't know how it happens, but suspect it's some sort of black magic.

The point I'm making with all this is to take a bit of time to **make a home** your own before you run straight in with your well-labelled boxes. It's so worth putting in a couple of days of forward thinking and planning so that by the time you do lay your duvet out and line your shoes up in colour order (ha!), you feel a little bit more like it's your place and can settle in a lot faster.

Items like these blankets, fluffy cushions, **small cosy lamps**, fairy lights (I kid you not, my house is almost entirely lit by fairy lights), photo frames (with friends and family in of course) and **rugs** make such a difference. If you really want to push the boat out, bits and pieces like art on the wall, cute wicker magazine racks, decorative **mirrors** and plants really, really can take a place from house to home.

A HOME FOR TWO HAPPY CLAMS

Once the adventures (and oh my, there were adventures) of the Gal-Pal Palace came to an end, it was time for me to play house with my fiancé and move into a small, but perfectly formed, city-centre apartment. Located in the heart of Liverpool, only five minutes from my office and ten minutes from all our favourite haunts, we were two happy clams. It was a new build, so there was no need to paint or revamp – we felt like the cats that got the cream.

The big setting-up-home lesson I learnt at this stage in my life was about storage. With space being a major premium, we had to find pretty creative ways to squeeze all our ~~junk~~ very important and crucial things in.

Here are three tips to help you with this:

● **Think vertically.** Can you hang shelves and hooks? Think about displaying pretty kitchenware (like glasses, cups, plates, etc.) on shelves, hang pots and pans from hooks on rails, and consider mounted racks. This will save you a heap of cupboard space and might be the difference between a cluttered, messy kitchen and a happy, goddess baking zone!

● **Use clear boxes and vacuum-pack bags.** Slide clear boxes (some even come on wheels) under your bed and use them for things you don't use daily but want easy access to (mine are full of handbags and clutches). By having them in clear boxes, you can easily see what you have and you keep dust and debris at bay (and also spiders! They get everywhere and my life is a constant battle against them). Vacuum-pack bags are also fantastic for tight spaces. I use mine to rotate my clothes. So in the winter I have all my floaty summer dresses and shorts in them, and then in the summer I pack away the woolly jumpers, tights and thick dresses. All you do is pop your garments in (you can also use it for blankets, duvets and bedding which is great), seal the bag, pop your vacuum cleaner's nozzle in the special hole, suck out all the air and, like magic, the bag shrinks!

● **Consider functional storage.** An aunt of mine used to have a foot stool that you could lift the top off and there was a secret cubby to keep toys and videos in (thank goodness for slimline DVDs these days!). If you look for it, there are plenty of ways to incorporate items that have a primary function as well as storage ability into your home. At the very least, a few pleasant-looking wicker baskets and hampers are a great way to stylishly clear away clutter.

A SUBURBAN HOME

After our lovebird apartment, we bit the bullet and put a deposit down on a proper, grown-up, three-bedroom house in the suburbs. Whilst it was a super-exciting time for me, I was also really concerned about how I would find the money and the know-how to fill the place!

My first piece of advice is to take advice. Sounds so obvious, I know! I also know that listening to your mum/aunt/grandma bend your ear about all the things they think are important can wear a little thin sometimes. On this occasion though, listen. Chances are they've already bought their homes and will have some golden tips to steer you in the right direction.

When we bought our house we were considered to be very young home owners, so naturally we'd not had time to save up big reserves of cash to shell out on all the things a home needs. In our rented apartment, basic things you need, like a fridge, hoover, washing machine and furniture, were all provided. In our new place, we were starting from scratch.

Before we'd moved in, I'd spent weeks flicking through glossy home-style magazines and trawling through interior design blogs! When we moved in, it was a little bit of a shock to see that my new home was actually a higgledy-piggle of second-hand items our family had kindly donated. My parents gave us an old fridge, an older sofa set and an even older than that TV. My grandma and granddad let us have their old dining table and chairs, and my aunts supplied an abundance of lovelies by way of cushions, crockery and all things in between.

It wasn't the dream home from the magazines, nor was it the uber-stylish living quarters from the blogs I'd gazed at, but it was mine. It was a mishmash of love and generosity, and with some creative upcycling, a few cans of spray paint and a good clean, it was perfect.

Over the years, bit by bit we have replaced the old with the new and styled our house into the home we wanted, but I will never forget the way my family gathered around and helped me. As my sisters, cousins and daughter grow up, I hope to do the same for them when their time comes.

Although it might not suit your colour scheme or you might be a bit bummed that it isn't exactly what you want, if you are on a tight budget, don't be snooty; gracefully and gratefully accept offers from friends and family.

If you don't have friends and family to hand (half of our family live quite a distance away), don't be shy about looking around charity shops, auctions and car boot sales. There are some completely amazing projects I have seen on Pinterest that involve old furniture and a few crafty moves to totally transform things! Some of my favourite things in my house are the bits and pieces that I've picked up from markets or vintage sales and put my own stamp on. Spray paint is usually my preferred method – it's affordable, fast and easy. My kind of DIY!

NO BETTER THING TO BUILD

However you decide to set up your home, no matter what type of home that is or who you're setting up with, I think that if you go into it with a positive mindset and think of it as an exciting project, do as much research as possible, be as creative as you can and have a willing attitude, you're going to make it a great place to live.

Setting up a home is a wonderful experience. Once you have it how you like it, you can shut the door, tuck yourself away and be content in your own perfect place in the world.

Remember to cherish the days when your dad scrapes your paint work as he helps carry in your sofa bed, or the moments where you and your friends test out eighteen different shades of cream paint, because you will definitely look back on them with fondness. You were building your home, and in my opinion, there is no better thing to build than that.

♡

BE CONTENT
IN YOUR OWN
PERFECT PLACE
IN THE WORLD.

♡ ♡ ♡

PRETTIFYING YOUR ROOM

If the previous section on setting up your home doesn't apply to you yet, because you're living safely cocooned in the home of your parents, then this next section in my oh so fabulous book (is it? Please say it is!) is for you.

If you haven't yet flown the nest but you do have an interest in making spaces personal, creative and beautiful, this chapter is for you. We are going to discuss a few of the ways you can make your bedroom the most wonderful place to relax, have fun and be inspired. Keep reading lovely one, I've got just what you need.

Now, I'm assuming that your parents or the people you live with are very liberal and will allow you to do quite a lot with your room. I'm going to be talking about gentle DIY activities and making changes to wall colours, and I know a fair few parents or landlords might object to that. If certain parts don't apply to you, just skip past them.

When I was a teenager, I had to beg my dad for months just to let me Blu Tack a poster to the wall. He thought that when I peeled it down I would pull the paintwork off and make the room 'unsightly'. I spent hours talking him round (goodness knows why those posters were so important to me!) and eventually he said yes. I hope he never reads this paragraph because do you know what? He was right. I did ruin the paintwork when I switched them about, and they did look messy and rubbish. I had too much pride to tell him though and so this section is going to be full of non-rubbish-posters-with-Blu-Tack ideas that you hopefully won't have to beg anyone to allow. Quick, sneaky pro tip though, if you are gaga for posters, frame them and hang the frames. It looks much cleaner and as you tire of each poster, just switch another one into the frame. Yay!

A clean slate

The very first thing you need to do before making any big changes is to clean, tidy and **organise your bedroom**. By this, I don't mean just a quick whip around with the vacuum and a shoving of stuff under the bed (I know how tempting that is, I'm an absolute fiend for what I call 'a quick once over'), but a big, proper sort out. Go through your wardrobe and chuck out or donate things you no longer wear. **Clean out drawers and cupboards**. Change your sheets. Vacuum the floor and polish the surfaces. Once you have this perfectly ordered room, you have a clean slate and you are ready to set off on the exciting adventure of prettifying (very real word there), transforming and upgrading!

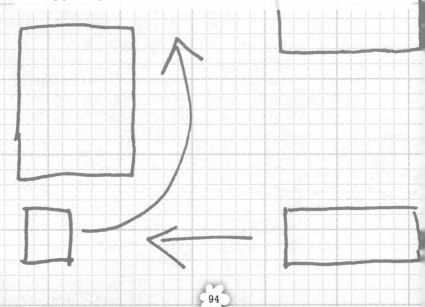

Consider your space

Once you are confident that you have cleaned, tidied and cleared away enough, open your windows, **let the room breathe a bit and assess the space**. Is your furniture arranged in the best possible way? Could you make any changes to allow more light in or to make the room seem bigger? Do you have space to create a reading nook or a beauty zone? A good idea is to draw the footprint of the room (just roughly) on a piece of paper and bit by bit add furniture in different sequences. It will give you an idea as to what works and what doesn't before you commit to dragging your dressing table across the carpet. When moving things about, make sure you **consider which way the door opens**, leaving yourself enough space to easily get in and out, and that your furniture and electronics are in convenient places for plug sockets. I keep toying with the idea of moving my bed to the other wall, but then I realise there are no sockets in that area and so lamps, chargers and fairy lights would be a bit of an issue. These things sound boring but they are important. A life without fairy lights wrapped round a bed frame is no life at all! Obviously, I'm being dramatic there, but you know, be sensible.

If you are struggling to think past the way your bedroom is already arranged, consider inviting friends over to get their input, **look online** at some interior design websites or as always, turn to good old faithful Pinterest and see what it has to offer. Sometimes (like in my room) it's hard to make big changes, but little things like switching a chair and a laundry hamper around or moving a rug into a different position can make all the difference. Remember, if you are going to make big changes, check with whoever owns the house that it's alright and if things are heavy, **ask for help**. Also, wear shoes! All too many times I have been lugging big ol' heaps of junk around and dropped it on my foot or stubbed my toes. The pain is very real and I've learnt my lesson!

Walls, walls, walls!

One of the biggest changes you can make to a room is to paint or paper the walls. I know this is a big job but it really does not need to be too expensive, especially if you are a dab hand at DIY. If you have a smaller room, opt for light, cool tones of paint colour and keep things simple. Busy patterns can make a room feel smaller. A fresh lick of paint (why is this a phrase? Who licks paint?) can totally transform a room and give it a new vibe.

If you have enough in the budget, new wallpaper is a super fun option. When we had our swirly pink paper (which you might have seen in my videos), I very sneakily stuck little gems all over it. Nothing fancy, just the plastic sticky-back ones you can buy in craft stores – where the pattern lent itself to it, I would dot a little sparkle. It's not very obvious at all but when the light hits, the gems twinkle and it looks really special. It's the small touches! If you are sharing a room, either do this when nobody is looking (hehe) or ask if they don't mind first – especially as wallpaper can be quite an expense! If you are looking for something that has the appearance of wallpaper but without the cost, you could try stencilling or painting something more personal. I have seen a lorra lorra chevron and block-stripe ideas on my favourite home-style blogs lately, and it looks like all you need to do is map out where you want everything (using a metre ruler and pencil), apply the masking tape and grab your paintbrush! I think that sounds like a really great frugal alternative and much less messy than paste and paper. Win–win!

Lastly for walls (I promise I have other things to talk about!), if the homeowner would prefer you not to paint or wallpaper, decals can offer a great solution. They are reusable stickers that don't damage walls when you peel them off – hurrah! They come in all kinds of shapes, sizes, words, patterns and look so adorable. They're not at all hard to find online, but unfortunately I haven't seen too many in shops in the UK. Definitely worth a Google search though!

Light it up!

Right, OK, you've tidied, cleared, cleaned, maybe painted, and you are wondering what to do next. At this point, I would tackle the lighting. First, ensure you are making the very most of your natural light. Remove anything big that might be blocking windows and open your curtains or blinds as far as they will go. Sunlight is your friend. It is beautiful, good for you and free – hurrah! Secondly, add small, soft lights. We have so many little lights in each room that it is rare for us to switch on the big main ceiling light. I feel like main lights give a very harsh light that isn't conducive to feeling cosy and relaxed, which, let's face it, is what I want to be 99 per cent of the time!

If I could illuminate my entire house solely with fairy lights, I would. I actually almost have! We have them in the office, the lounge, our bedroom, Darcy's bedroom and the hallway. I think fairy lights are the most magical things in this modern-day world. These long strings of tiny, dotted, colourful lights create enough glow to see and be seen, but not enough to glare or bother you. They are utter perfection. I particularly like how portable and practical they are. You can display them almost anywhere with ease. If you have a bedframe that you can wrap things around, pop them on that. Or I like to drape them over mirrors for a really sweet, twinkly effect. Also, they are the perfect selfie light, and what's not to love about that?!

👑 **Top tip:** Make sure, when you buy your fairy lights, that they're LED lights. These bulbs don't tend to overheat and are much safer. Never leave the room for long periods of time with them on, either. I've never had an issue with mine, but it's better to be safe than sorry.

Fairy lights might not be your thing (who are these people though? Seriously). Lamps, on the other hand, surely will be. Lamps produce a softer hue than ceiling lights and are a much more effective option if you are trying to achieve a calm and chilled-out atmosphere. At the moment, I am really into lamps that don't look like lamps. No, I haven't gone mad – I mean non-traditional shapes or ideas for lamps. My friend Daniel has a lamp that looks like amber tree sap and that always really pleases me. Basically, if it glows, twinkles or very gentle illuminates, I want it. It's been joked about in the past that I have a 'lighting problem'. I prefer to call it a 'collection'.

To create the illusion of more space in your little bedroom, turn to mirrors. If you position them well, they are incredibly effective. If you don't have the wall space for mirrors, think outside the box. Are you able to put a mirror on the back of your door? Could you replace standard wardrobe doors with mirrored ones? I have sliding, mirrored wardrobe doors across the length of my room and it really makes it feel twice as big. Plus, bedroom dance parties are the absolute best!

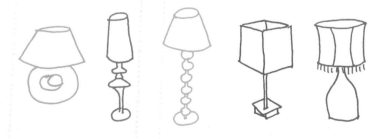

Mix it up!

A really quick and low maintenance way to prettify your room is to change and mix up the style of your bedding. As we talked about in Setting Up Home, supermarkets and high-street stores have some absolutely gorgeous and very affordable sets that you could nip out, pick up, pop on and voilà – instant update! Personally I love the idea of changing bedding styles with the seasons. I have a dedicated set for Christmas, and this year might hunt down something nice and bright for the summer. Since the bed is usually a focal point in the bedroom, it's a very obvious and simple way to make a big, noticeable change. If buying brand new bedding sets isn't an option for you, dot on some bright scatter cushions or a bright throw blanket and you have a mini-update in moments. You could even get really crafty and make some cushion covers out of any old fabric you have to hand or out of unloved shirts and dresses. They are easy, affordable and have a lovely personal vibe too. More on this idea in the next section!

Now that we have discussed a few practical, heavy-duty ways to make a difference in your bedroom, let's look at some really cute and fun things you can do to jazz up your space. A lot of these ideas are things you can either enjoy doing alone or make an evening out of with friends and family!

Selfie wall

A 'selfie wall' is a spot in your bedroom that is customised for the perfect selfie. To make one, find a big bit of spare wall that isn't adorned with mirrors, frames, posters, etc. and that has good light, either from a window or lamp. Take a test-shot selfie so you can see how much space you will need and which parts of the wall need to be customised. Once you have worked this out, add fairy lights, polaroid snaps, feather garlands and/or anything else that tickles your pickle. You could even have a little box of goodies that you could use to switch it up when you fancy something different. Think of it as your own personal photobooth and style it accordingly. I love the idea of using gold glitter card and cutting out stars to have in the background.

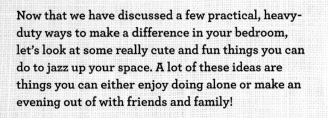

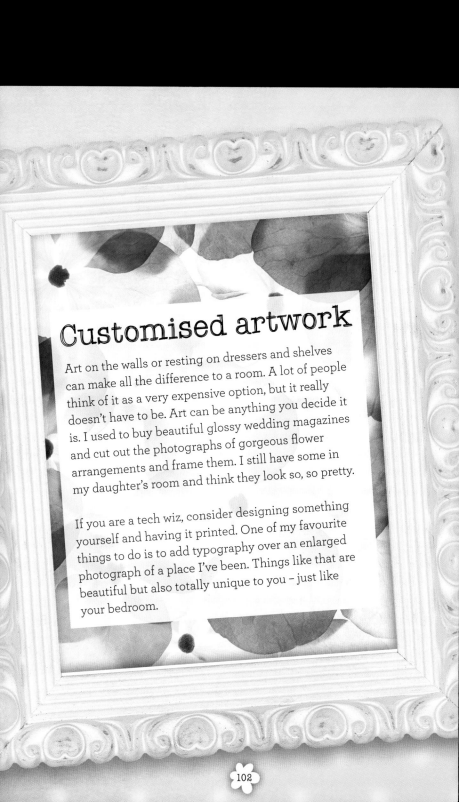

Customised artwork

Art on the walls or resting on dressers and shelves can make all the difference to a room. A lot of people think of it as a very expensive option, but it really doesn't have to be. Art can be anything you decide it is. I used to buy beautiful glossy wedding magazines and cut out the photographs of gorgeous flower arrangements and frame them. I still have some in my daughter's room and think they look so, so pretty.

If you are a tech wiz, consider designing something yourself and having it printed. One of my favourite things to do is to add typography over an enlarged photograph of a place I've been. Things like that are beautiful but also totally unique to you – just like your bedroom.

Treats hamper

In my humble little opinion, there is nothing more delightful than a wicker hamper. I have a habit of spray-painting every wicker thing I find (I always go for pastel colours but you could go with anything you like) and matching it to the theme of my room. A lovely idea for any bedroom is to have a treats hamper. Fill it with beauty products, pamper bits, bath fizzes, food treats (let's face it, you want to put crisps, sweets and chocolate in there don't you?), DVDs, cosy PJs and magazines. Whenever you have a rubbish day, some spare time or have friends over, pop out the treats hamper and you have a readymade evening of relaxation waiting for you!

Happy jars

Happy jars, it just makes me happy to say it. Happy jars! Happy jars! See? Ha.

A happy jar is a trinket you can keep in your room that you put your happy moments in. Take a large glass jar and fill it with ticket stubs, secret notes, love letters or memories you have jotted down. Do this as regularly as possible and also ask anyone who comes into your room to leave you a little note too. Then, when you feel like it, you can open up the jar, tip out all the lovelies and really enjoy reading through and seeing what a wonderful time you have had or how well cared for you are. It's the perfect pick-me-up on a rainy day and sometimes it's just what you need. To really add to it, decorate the jar with lace, ribbons, stickers, gems or whatever you have to hand and like the look of.

Pegged photos

Taking your beloved photographs off your phone, laptop or computer and actually displaying them is a great way to jazz up your bedroom. It might seem like a bit of a hassle but, actually, the process of clicking through them all and reminding yourself of all the lovely things you've done is really therapeutic and bound to put a smile on your face. There are lots of ways to display them in your room, but my favourite is hanging them on twine with little pegs. My friend Hazel has this kind of look going on in her room and I always find myself gazing at all the snaps when I go in there.

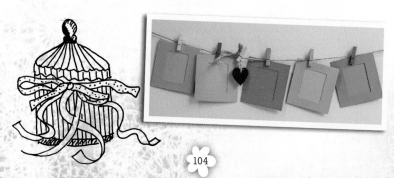

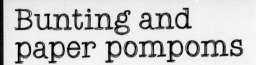

Bunting and paper pompoms

Decorating your bedroom with sweet bunting and giant paper pompoms is a super-easy way to make things pretty without altering anything drastic (parents – you're welcome!). You can find out how to make both of these things in the Crafts section. I recommend taking yourself off to Pinterest or to look at some craft blogs to get some palette and pattern inspiration.

Chalkboard door

Lately on crafty interior blogs I have seen a lorra lorra chalkboard paint. Chalkboard-framed noticeboards, chalkboard playzones, chalkboard cupboard doors, anything that is flat! A nice idea for a bedroom would be to chalkboard paint the back of your bedroom door (either the whole thing or a smaller section) and use it as a space to leave yourself little reminders, to do lists or positive affirmations to make you smile. Chalkboard paint is easy to come by, just make sure you read the instructions and give it enough drying time in between coats!

I hope some of the above ideas were useful to you! Whatever you decide to do to your bedroom, whether you take just one or every single idea from this chapter, do it with optimism and a good attitude.

Sometimes things will work and look incredible and sometimes you'll do things and think, 'Oopsie!' It doesn't matter, you can keep at it, try again and be proud of your efforts.

The key things to take away from this are:

- Give everywhere a thorough clean and tidy before you begin

- Consider a fresh coat of paint

- Add soft touches like cushion and blankets for fun pops of colour

- Create great lighting and sprinkle as many fun and creative touches about as you possibly can

These are the things that really make a room stand out as special.

Good Luck!

♡

♡

♡

♡

♡

CRAFTS

My love affair with arts and crafts began before I can even remember. In fact, I don't recall a time in my life when I wasn't in love with them. My darling mum, Jane, had a great love for making beautiful things – as well as a talent for business and a keen eye for style. When I was teeny tiny, she started building a business and was soon running and managing craft fairs all around the country. I remember how she lovingly made all kinds of pressed-flower creations, like framed pictures, lockets, rings and bookmarks, which she'd sell at her fairs.

For my creative young soul, it was an inspiring environment to grow up in and I would spend a great many hours sitting with her, cutting and gluing and using tweezers to gently lift and slot delicate petals into place. I loved the development process of a project and then seeing it in all its finished glory, knowing how much love and labour had made it that way. It was a pleasure to be around a person with so much fizz and energy for crafting, and it was a joy to be given so much artistic freedom. Like I said, I can't ever remember a time when I didn't want to just make things. Sadly, my smart and gifted mother lost her battle with cancer when I was seven but her love for making still lives on in me.

So this section, which will offer fun projects, tips and ideas for you to do yourselves, will be dedicated especially to her. I think she would like that a lot.

Easy-peasy fabric bunting

Bunting can come in a million, zillion different colours and patterns, and it can be really easy or difficult to make it. Since I am not a skilled sewer (despite having owned more sewing machines than any one gal would ever need), we're going to opt for the simplest set of instructions. The type of bunting we are making will look rustic and shabby-chic – this is what I like to tell myself anyway!

YOU WILL NEED:

Fabric (pattern and colour of your choice, but natural cotton and linen work best and manmade fabrics like nylon or polyester can be tricky to work with)

Scissors

Pinking shears

Needle and thread (WonderWeb or fabric glue will work as an alternative)

Ribbon

Stiff card

A ruler

A pencil

TO MAKE:

1 Using your ruler, pencil, card and scissors, carefully cut out an isosceles triangle to use as a template for your bunting.

2 Place the card template on the fabric, draw around it in pencil and cut out, with pinking shears, as many triangles as you see fit (the more you cut out, the longer your strip of bunting will be).

3 Lay your ribbon out flat and place your pre-cut triangles at even spaces along it.

4 One by one, sew the triangles onto the ribbon, with the longest point facing down. You can either do this step by hand or with a sewing machine.

5 If sewing isn't your thing, you can use WonderWeb and an iron, or fabric glue.

6 Once you have adhered your triangles to the ribbon, you're all set! Drape your bunting everywhere for a pretty, countryside vibe and be pleased with your handiwork!

Bonus: If you have no fabric supplies and hate sewing, use paper, ribbon and a stapler for something a little different but still super-easy!

GENUINE POLISHED BOXWOOD

W.H. HAYDEN & CO. LT

Re-shaped crayons

Re-shaped wax crayons are perfect to use as party favours, pencil case novelties or as handmade stocking fillers. They are a cute and easy craft you can make with very few resources.

Wax crayons
A silicone ice-cube shape tray (we have hearts and flowers at home)
A knife
An oven

1 Pre-heat oven to 200°C.

2 Peel any paper or wrapping off your crayons.

3 Chop each crayon into tiny pieces, to around half a centimetre long.

4 Place the pieces of crayon in to the silicone mould (block colours or mix them up to make swirly new colours!).

5 Leave in the oven for 6 minutes and remove.

6 Once the wax is hard and the tray cool, pop out your new creations!

A gold-tipped feather garland

A delicate string of natural-coloured feathers with a hint of glimmer is a beautiful and unique addition to your bedroom or office, and it's easy-peasy lemon-squeezy to make.

YOU WILL NEED:

Feathers (I prefer store-bought ones as the ones found in the
  park, on the floor, are always a bit yukky and full of germs)
Cotton, or fishing wire
A small piece of card
Gold spray paint
Scissors
Old newspaper or a protective mat

TO MAKE:

1 Lay a feather on the protective mat and about half way up, lay the card on top of the feather, leaving the bottom tip exposed and the rest hidden under the card.

2 After reading the spray paint canister instructions, spray the bottom of the feather.

3 Turn the feather over and repeat on the other side – do this to all feathers.

Cut the cotton to the length you would like your garland to be.

4 Once the feathers have dried, tie them by the stalk to the cotton and voilà, you have a dainty adornment to display wherever you like!

Personal map frame

The perfect present for a best friend or partner, a personal map frame is a memento of the special places you have been to together, or the geographic areas that have made an impact on your life. Now this one is really quick and easy!

YOU WILL NEED:

A multi-frame (you know the ones with lots of windows to pop your pictures in)

Maps of special places you have been to or that mean something to you (if you can't buy them, print them out)

Scissors

A pencil

TO MAKE:

Using the mount of the frame as a guide, with a pencil, draw on the map the area you want. Cut out the maps and put them in the frames. So easy!

When I did this I used a frame with three compartments, and I used maps of Liverpool, London and Los Angeles because these are all cities I have made amazing memories in with my friends. Since this is such a quick craft, it makes the perfect 'oh no, I forget it's their birthday and need to gift something quick' idea! Teehee.

Block-colour glass jars

If you have been an avid follower of my blog (thank you), you may remember back in February 2013 when I upcycled glass and turned food jars into cute pastel vases. I love that this craft lets you take an everyday household object and use it to create something that's unique and fits any colour scheme in your home. You don't have to use the jars to hold flowers either, they can be used to home your make-up brushes or as super-pretty desk holders for your pens. With that many possibilities, what are you waiting for?

YOU WILL NEED:

Clean and dry glass jars
Acrylic paint
Newspaper or a protective mat

TO MAKE:

1 Squeeze a generous amount of acrylic paint into your glass jar.

2 Hold, twist and move the jar in such a way that the paint glides around and covers all inner areas of the jar.

3 Drain out the excess paint, leave to dry and you're done!

I like to do this with a few jars at a time, in varying shades of the same colour to make for a fun display. If you give this craft a whirl, tweet me your pictures. ♡

Giant paper pompoms

Giant paper pompoms have been a fixture in my house for some years. They make great additions to bedroom decor and look sweet as decorations at parties and other celebrations. I like to make a range of sizes, and since this craft is so flexible, I think you will too.

YOU WILL NEED:

A packet of tissue paper in your colour of choice
Easily bendable craft wire
Cotton, or fishing wire
Scissors

TO MAKE:

1 Take eight sheets of paper and place them on top of each other (I tend not to measure things out – if I want big pompoms I just use an entire sheet from the pack, or half a sheet for smaller ones. You'll soon get the hang of sizing!).

2 Make a concertina of the stacked sheets of tissue in one-inch folds, down the length of the paper, as if making a fan.

3 Once your whole batch is folded, wrap the craft wire around the middle of the paper and twist the wire to secure it.

4 Using your scissors, round off the edges of the fan (this will make it look soft and pretty at the end).

5 Open out the fan and, one by one, separate each layer of tissue paper. Gradually, it will start to look like a big puff ball. Keep going until you have a full sphere of tissuey goodness.

6 Attach the cotton or fishing wire to the little bit of twisted wire in the middle and hang wherever you so desire. B-e-a-u-t-i-f-u-l!

The year I went craft gaga and loved it!

After graduating from university I found myself in an oh-me-oh-my-so-so-so boring office job at a recruitment agency. I didn't enjoy it, I had very little disposable income and my university social life was over, so I had a lot of spare time.

One day, a leaflet landed on the doormat advertising adult-learning evening courses. Night school, basically! There were lists and lists of all sorts of usual things like 'Chinese Cookery', 'Salsa Dancing' and 'IT Skills', but the one that tickled my pickle was 'Beading for Beginners'. Since I'd always had a creative streak, and at that time it wasn't being used, I decided I may as well fork out the £48 and go along to the first week to see what it was all about.

The course was run by a lady with long brown hair and an array of twinkling, beaded beauties on her wrists, neck, ears and head. She was a beading enthusiast and was keen to teach us everything she knew so that we too would be sucked into the very, very addictive world that she loved so much.

In our first lesson, we were taught spiral stitch and, in our second, ladder. We used teeny tiny Japanese glass-seed beads and a thread called Nymo to make our intricate creations. When she arrived each week, she would tip a clear plastic storage box over on the table and out would spill hundreds of small clear packets of beads for us to choose from. There were acid greens, blood reds, candy pinks, shimmering golds and everything in between. Some had iridescent effects and some were matt, but the joy of it was sifting through, picking bags up, holding them to the light and deciding if they were for you. It brought me such joy to look through those little gem-like beads and then spend a peaceful two hours working with them.

That Christmas I gave just about everyone I knew a beaded creation! I'm not sure they were as impressed as I was, but I think the thing I learnt from that course wasn't peyote stitch or threading on silver-plated clasps, but how much joy I got out of crafting. I loved sitting still, with no screens or technology – just your hands and your mind building something beautiful, and using only your own energy, skill and patience. It is so therapeutic to pour your time and love into something like that, and then have a tangible outcome at the end. Something you can hold and feel and see and touch, and knowing that your hard work had made it.

I hope that after reading this you are inspired to put down your phone or close your laptop and feel the same joy I do and my mother did when we make things. In a day and age where everything is instant and everything is rushed, take a moment to step back, work at a slower pace and enjoy each moment of it – it's good for the soul, I'm sure.

It all started many years ago when I was in Year Seven and Mrs Davis, the Home Economics teacher, set us the task of baking a very standard, very simple sponge cake. All we had to do was measure out the ingredients at home, bring them to school in zip-lock baggies, mix them, put them in the oven and, hey presto, there's a cake! How could that possibly go wrong?

I'll tell you how. Flour and icing sugar look *exactly* the same. You put those sneaky white powders in see-through bags, without a label, and you're instantly in a pickle. You put icing sugar instead of flour in your cake and now you're in even more of a pickle. I'll spare you the details but, basically, the 'cake' went pop! And so did my enthusiasm for baking. I realise this doesn't sound earth-shattering, but for a timid 11-year-old with issues about failing (let's pretend I don't still have those, eh?) it was a lot to take on.

As I've grown and matured, I've tried to find my way back to feeling joy in the kitchen, but I've never quite arrived there. Sure, I've attempted cakes again. There was the time I tried to make Matt a Spider Man cake with red and blue layers of sponge. I'll never understand where I went wrong but the red and blue layers were more green and brown and the delicate black iced web I'd planned for the top, well... no. Just no. It was a disaster.

Then I moved on to biscuits. I had seen some incredible photographs of Nutella sandwich cookies and thought I'd give them a whirl. I bought all of the ingredients. I so, so carefully measured them out on my retro scales and followed the recipe to the letter. Again, I'm not sure quite where I went awry but when my sister Tiyana described them as 'little choc rocks', I knew I'd not quite mastered it yet.

When my daughter was born, I thought it might be time to try again. Ooohhh, we could bake together, Mama and Darcy, cooking up a storm. How sweet! Well, storm was the right word there, when I forgot to check the oven (toddlers are very distracting you know) and the fairy cakes turned black as rain clouds.

And so I've given up. I'm throwing in the towel... the tea towel! I've decided some people are cut out for cookie cutters and some are not. I, clearly, am not.

In this chapter, we're going to look at yummy treats you can make for friends and family WITHOUT having to bake. No long lists of ingredients, no complicated cooking instructions, no fuss – just lovely, fun foodie ideas that anyone can do. Even me.

CRISPIE TREATS

Melt chocolate in glass bowl in a microwave, taking it out to stir every few seconds to avoid the sugar crystallising. **Add puffed rice cereal.** Plop a spoonful or two into individual cake cases and chill until they turn hard.

Oh Louise, really? You're putting the most standard treat ever in a book and you're not even telling us to melt things the way you're supposed to – over a bowl of boiling steamy water? Yes, that's right kids, I am. BUT, there's an extra instruction. *Sassy head move at the nay-sayers* **Add edible glitter.** A sprinkle of glitter can make anything wonderful.

Pro (ha!) tip:

Never, ever 'treat yourself' to one teeny tiny teaspoon of the mixture whilst it's warm and gooey. You'll wind up two hours later with chocolate all over your face and a giant empty mixing bowl resting on your tummy as you stare mindlessly at trash TV, wondering what it was you were supposed to do that day. Not that I've ever done that ahahahahahahaha *nervous laughter and shifty eyes* hahahaha. Ha. Let's move on.

CHOCOLATE-DIPPED POPPING STRAWBERRIES

Melt chocolate as above (or using whatever method you want really, I'm not the Melting Police). Pour the molten goodness (the melted chocolate) into a sweet little bowl and place in the middle of a larger plate. Add washed, uncut **strawberries** to the outside of the plate. Tip a packet of **popping candy** into a teenier bowl (see how profesh this is?!) and add to plate.

You've just set yourself up for a reeeaalllll gooooodd time!

Dip strawberry in melted chocolate, dip now-gooey strawberry in popping candy, put all of that in your mouth, shut your eyes and be glad you read this magnificent chapter.

You are welcome my friend, you are welcome.

Pro (ha!) tip:

Once you have washed the strawberries, give them a little dry on a paper towel. Water droplets and melted chocolate don't really mix well and you'll be glad of this step in the long run.

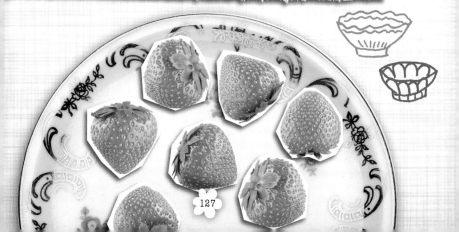

SMOOTHIE LOLLIES

Smoothie lollies are the kind of treats that look incredibly impressive, when really even I can make them. There is something really satisfying about sitting in the garden and very casually saying, 'Oh, I almost forgot! I have homemade smoothie lollies in the freezer, who'd like one?' Hostess with the mostess times a million.

Buy some **ice-lolly moulds** (either online or from supermarkets – we have about six billion – I can't stop buying them!) and a carton of your favourite smoothie OR go cray cray and make your own blended creation. **Pour the smoothie into the moulds and freeze until hard.** The end. (Told ya it was easy!)

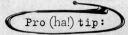

Pro (ha!) tip:

Be careful not to pour the smoothie right to the very top of the mould because as liquid freezes, it expands, and you don't want an overflow!

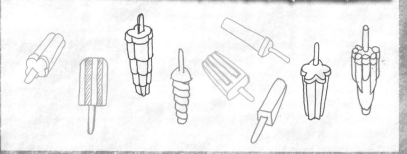

CANDY BARK OR 'CHOCOLATE PIZZA'

About a year ago two of my siblings (Ben and Hollie) came to stay with me for a few days whilst our parents (my dad is with their mum) went on holiday to India. I wanted to make sure they had a really fun time at my house, so I planned on giving them lots of little treats and, after seeing 'Candy Bark' on Pinterest, we decided to give it a go.

All you do to make it is melt a large family-size bar of chocolate (this should have been called the 'melt chocolate a lot' chapter!), pour it onto baking paper that is laid on a flat surface (like the work counter or a plate) and sprinkle on whatever yummies you like! We opted for things like gummy sweets and dolly mixtures in white chocolate, but I've seen really interesting concoctions with things like dark chocolate and salted pretzel pieces!

Once the chocolate has hardened in the fridge, snap it into shards and serve. Ben thought the shards looked like pizza slices, and so in our house 'Chocolate Pizza' is a thing.

Pro (ha!) tip:

This makes a lovely yet super inexpensive gift, and can be easily colour themed to suit events or seasons.

And so, there we have it. Possibly the worst chapter about 'baking' ever written. I hope and pray Mary Berry never, ever reads this. If you do, Mary, I'm sorry. Also, I think your blazers are always fabulous.

I think the key message to take away from all of this is not to worry. Sometimes you excel and sometimes you don't, and that's alright.

Nobody can be perfect at everything and nobody is. Those people who make perfectly even cupcakes (hello ZoeChummy!) might not be able to do something you can do.

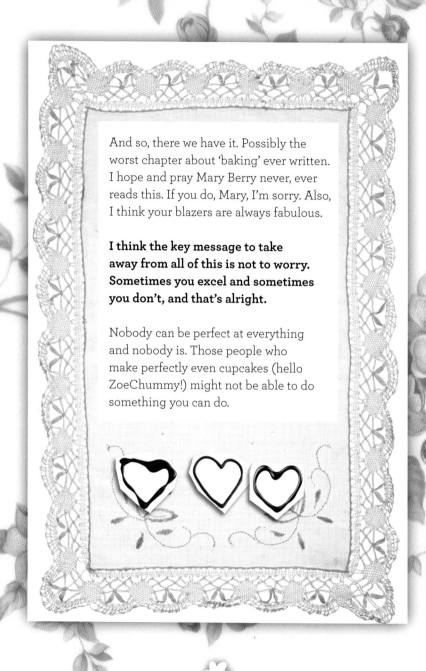

AS LONG AS
YOU ARE
HAVING
FUN AND
TRYING
YOUR BEST,
THAT'S
ALL THAT
MATTERS.

Need to Knows

SURVIVING EDUCATION 134

BULLYING 152

ONLINE SAFETY 160

BODY CONFIDENCE 176

COMFORT ZONES 190

SURVIVING
EDUCATION

"Your school days are the best days of your life"

– Anonymous

Wrong. So, so wrong.

I've rather mockingly called this chapter 'Surviving Education', and for that I feel a little guilty. Before we get into the tips and LOLs (by the way, is saying 'LOL' in my first-ever published book incredibly lame? Somebody humour me and laugh at at least one thing in it please! Ahaha <-- Oh, I did it myself there. OK, this bracket chat needs to stop now), I want to take a moment to be the tiniest bit serious, if I may.

Education is a privilege.

I know day to day, when you're pulling on 60 denier tights at 7am and wondering what excuses you can give for not doing your homework (left it at your gran's/the printer won't print/your baby brother hid it, etc.), it might not feel like one, but as you read this chapter, spare a thought for your counterparts in areas of the world who would love to have the gift of education like you do. The very fact that you are able to read this book at all is a luxury, when you think about it. You can read. Someone taught you to do that. The person who taught you was taught by somebody else. I'm going to presume that the majority of people reading this are women (although hello boys, you are most welcome here too) and so I would ask you to just take a moment to remember that a great deal of the women in the world today are not privy to the educational opportunities that you are. I hope that as we take steps to make the world a better place, this will begin to change.

Now, not forgetting that poignant note, but setting it aside for a few minutes whilst I go back to my gripes about 60 denier tights on winter mornings, let's talk about my education. The good, the bad and the ugly.

I began my learning journey at a local mixed-sex state school that my mum tried to entice me to by telling me that when she'd looked around there had been a fish tank with tadpoles in it. It worked, I was excited. So Mum and Dad dropped me off in my pristine little red and grey uniform and told a tearful little LouLou that they were nipping to the post office and would be back in ten minutes. They lied. It was hours. Hours and hours of waiting to be collected. Those blighters.

After a very short settling in period, I got the hang of it and enjoyed lower school. I had some pretty revered lunchtime duties (I was trusted with the prestigious position of looking after the school rabbit for a whole term. Oh me oh my, I felt grand about that) and made best friends with a little red-headed girl called Ruth who, when we were eight years old, made the greatest sacrifice a lower school friend could ever make – she gave me her cardigan at playtime when it was cold. Ruth, if ever you read this, thank you. One day I shall give you my cardigan in return. It is the circle of life.

Looking back, lower school was blissful. I'm not sure 4- to 9-year-olds are that challenging and I don't remember any of the work being terribly difficult either. Except that time they made me do 'estimations', the most pointless and frustrating of all maths lessons. I'm still annoyed about that. 'Estimate the length of one footstep.' WHY??? I digress.

I think the real survival challenge comes once you hit your teenage years at school. For me, this was spent at an all-girls private school. AKA hell on earth. Bit strong? Maybe. But have you ever spent seven years of your life trapped in a building with 650 hormonal women? Good grief, there's a survival challenge for you.

I quickly realised that in each day there would be wonderful bits (working on a topic you really love, laughing so hard with your friend in the courtyard that you pee yourself (true story)), horrible bits (being picked on by the mean girls, slipping over naked in the swimming pool changing rooms or finding your yoghurt has burst in your bag) and perfectly fine bits (assemblies, lessons, general school life). The key is to learn how to manage the horrible bits so that they feel 'perfectly fine', and then it's happy days. Maybe the people who tell you 'Your school days are the best days of your life' are the people who really mastered that skill.

In my opinion, your educational years are not made up of the greatest, most wonderful and perfect days that everyone says they'll be; they are great, but they are also incredibly challenging. This chapter is going to look at ways we can acknowledge that they are tough and talk about things you can do to ease those situations a little bit.

There are two things that are key to surviving education:

1. **Learning (and all that it encompasses).**

2. **People (all of them, oh jeez).**

LEARNING

It's time for tough Louise now. Learning is important. Face facts, you need to learn. It is critical to your future and the more you learn at school, the better your chances of success are later on in life. I'm sure this isn't a new fact for you to face, but have you ever questioned what that means? There are two big things in there that are worth examining – the words 'learn' and 'success'.

During my school days, I often felt that the emphasis during our lessons was on learning from text books or novels or from practical exercises in the laboratories. Obviously, I opted out of any home economics subjects (you read the Anti-Baking chapter right?) and I would have done almost anything to do as little PE as possible. I'll still never get over the time Laura Freeman accidentally thwacked me over the head with a hockey stick and our PE teacher just said, 'You'll live.' No compassion. Why are some PE teachers like this?!?! What was I talking about again? Ah, yes, learning.

As I have aged, I have realised that it's better to think of learning as a holistic experience rather than as an exercise in memorising facts out of a textbook, ready to regurgitate onto an exam paper in a sweaty school hall on a sunny afternoon. However, the art of surviving education is in part about learning to play the game and, to do that, you do have to spend a lot of time nervously scribbling answers onto a page in school halls in May (or whenever your exam season is). In the end, they lead to qualifications, which lead you to be afforded the careers you want, which in turn lead to you having the lifestyle you would prefer. That's the theory anyway.

Here are my top tips for 'playing the game' and surviving the learning part:

ORGANISE YOURSELF. This was and is my biggest life failing. If you struggle to keep up with homework diaries and assignment deadlines and ring binders full of lined A4, I well and truly relate. It's HARD. You have my sympathy and also my encouragement to try. If you conquer one thing in the organisation department, let it be a good diary. Keep careful track of what pieces of homework you have and what days you have to do it on. Use your diary to note exams and tests and also to schedule in revision time. Be realistic, give yourself enough time and, as you achieve something, tick it off or give yourself a little sticker – it's very rewarding. Diaries, in the end, also make for a nice keepsake to see all the good work you did in a year, so save and cherish them for when you're older. You might enjoy them.

ASK FOR HELP. If you are struggling, if you don't understand or if you want to know more, ask. Of course it's worth doing a little research yourself first, to see if you can find the answer but, if you are suffering, do not do it in silence. Your teachers are passionate about the subjects they teach so they're happy to help and want you to do well. Having been married to a teacher, I know how much he loves to help people learn and how he would never begrudge a student seeking his assistance. There is never any shame in admitting you don't know an answer, as long as you are striving to find it.

FIND YOUR TECHNIQUE. A lot of school learning seems to boil down to the end-of-year exams and that means remembering all you've been taught in the previous months and answering questions on it in an examination. Sounds easy perhaps, but when you are taking about ten different subjects, each with lots of subtopics, you'll quickly find there is an immense amount of information to cram into your brain in a short amount of time. Urgh. To help you do that, find a revision technique that works for you. Never mind that your friend has spent forty-five minutes making perfectly penned bullet points in eighty-five different coloured sparkle gel pens – that might not work for you, and it might end up being a massive waste of time, time you can't afford. Sadly for me, I didn't find my groove with this until my second year at university, where I failed seven out of ten summer exams in my first year (I fell in love with a boy in May, exams were in June. Oopsie) and had to re-sit the lot that August or lose my degree place.

Thank goodness, I worked out a revision method that made stuff stick (writing it out in short paragraphs and then explaining them to somebody who didn't know the subject, so kind of teaching someone else). I passed all seven exams with flying colours, kept my spot at uni and, if you're interested, five years later married that boy I fell in love with. So, learn from my mistake – if the gel pens and pointless attempts to make everything look pretty don't work for you, chuck them out, and spend your time finding ways to revise as efficiently and productively as possible.

I feel confident that if you can keep on top of the workload by staying organised, ask for help when you're stuck to keep things moving and have a good technique for revising, you are on track to surviving education pretty successfully!

PEOPLE

Whatever stage of education you're at in your life (even those of us who aren't 'in education' are still constantly learning), you will come across people you like, people who make your heart giddy with excitement, people who grate on you and people you downright dislike. **You can't change other people; you can only change your attitude towards them.**

From experience, the two groups of people I had to deal with whilst I was at school, college and university were other students and teachers. I think for many people 'boys' would be on that list too (or girls if they're your thang) but since I went to an all-girls school, it's hard for me to comment or advise there.

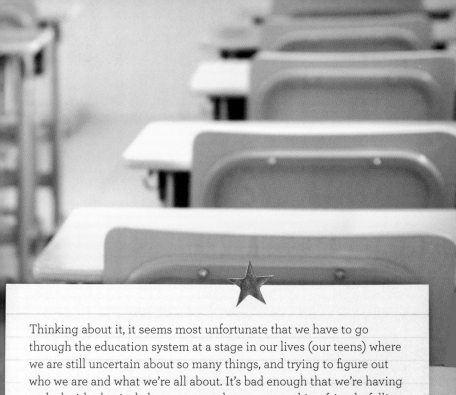

Thinking about it, it seems most unfortunate that we have to go through the education system at a stage in our lives (our teens) where we are still uncertain about so many things, and trying to figure out who we are and what we're all about. It's bad enough that we're having to deal with physical changes, crazy hormones, making friends, falling out with and then making up with said friends, boyfriends, girlfriends, bad friends and then, on top of that, learning stuff!!! With all that to deal with, education can seem really inconvenient and hard to keep up with. I'm going to give you a few of my own personal little tips for dealing with people so that, hopefully, it won't take up a huuuuuge amount of your brain space and then you really can focus a little more on the actual learning portion of your school/uni days. After all, that's what you're there for, isn't it?

friends

MAKING FRIENDS. This can be pretty daunting if you are entering a new environment, but if you are friendly (I know, it's easy to kind of shut down and keep yourself to yourself when you feel a bit shy or nervous but try to fight that), smile at people and start little chit-chats, you'll be on the road to chummies in no time! Try to find common ground or offer a little compliment to get things going.

FALL OUTS. Yep, it happens, especially at school and especially in your teenage years. Falling out with friends was the worst bit about school for me, particularly as I seemed to find myself in a group of very catty girls who made life rather miserable. If this is the situation you are in, leave this group now. It's really not worth your time to be constantly second-guessing yourself, worrying that you are being talked about behind your back or having to face nastiness. Don't make a big fuss, don't be a drama llama, just spend less time with them and more time with nicer people or in your own company. If, though, you've had a row with a good friend and you don't know how to fix it, my tip to you would be to talk face to face. It can often feel easier to text, PM, DM and all the other tippetty-tap-typey ways there are to chat, but real life face to face will always win out in these cases because you can read body language, sense the tone and overall have a better quality of communication. Basically, talk it out in real life and you are likely to resolve it much faster! Be mature, try very, very hard to consider their point of view (I know this is soooooooo difficult sometimes), and do your utmost not to raise your voice and swear.

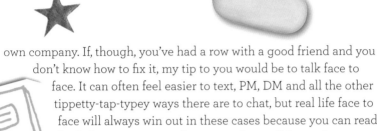

DECIDE IF YOU WANT TO RESOLVE AN ARGUMENT. If you don't, just walk away calmly and remain pleasant to the other party. If you do want to resolve it, talk it out, consider their side and then, when it's fixed, forgive and move on. No point dwelling and resenting. Anger is like a hot stone – if you hold onto it, it's your own hand that gets burnt.

GOOD FRIENDS. These are the people who you love dearly and who you know love you back. The kind of people who you can giggle with for hours, over nothing at all, share little jokes with, text the most ridiculous things to (the other day I text my friend Jack, saying: 'I just tried on white jeans. Very marshmallowy. Not sure a good look'). They are also the friends that you can sit and cry with if you need to. They are your support and your happies and your sillies, and they are to be treasured like gems in a shell-encrusted jewellery box. Good friends are hard to come by, so treat them well and keep hold of them.

Inevitably, you will go through phases of life where good friends drift away, bad friends make life hard and new friends come into view. It's natural. Some people will be with you forever, but some friendships will run their course and then people move on. That's honestly alright. Not everyone will be your BFF, no matter how much you plan your joint weddings and pledge that your children will be best friends, and their children will be best friends, and you'll live next door to each other for always and eternity.

As the old saying goes:

"Some friends are for reasons, some friends are for seasons and some friends are for life."

teachers/tutors/ lecturers

RESPECT. Mmm-hmm, behave. These people are doing their best to educate you, and so it doesn't matter if you like them or not, you should still be showing them your respect. This means not talking when they're talking, listening to what they have to say, doing as they ask, handing in assignments by the deadline so that they have time to mark them and, over all, being polite. I know that wasn't a particularly thrilling point but, having lived with a teacher, I know how important respect is to them and how much they care about their students. Nawww.

MEANIES. Teachers are people not robots. Some of them will be really nice people, and some, even though they chose to work with children/ young adults, are actually a bit mean. I'm sure all teachers now will hate me saying this but it's true, haha! I used to have a teacher who was positively beastly, a real cramp in my week! She called me 'Four Eyes' (because I wore glasses) and my ginger friend 'Carrot Top'. Of course this was all light-hearted humour (to her) but I noticed in class she would never pick me to answer a question, would give me unkind looks (I know, that sounds very flimsy, but Carrot Top noticed as well) and, in general, was really unpleasant. To make matters worse, when I was choosing my A-levels and considering picking her subject, she told me I didn't have the 'aptitude' for it. I got an A* at GCSE. No aptitude at all though. *wink*

My point is, in some very, very rare cases, you will find members of educational staff who are not treating you the way they should and in those cases you might consider the following:

- **Make absolutely sure you are being respectful to them, working hard and handing things in on time.** If you aren't, that would be a big clue as to why things aren't running smoothly for you.

- **Make a note of every incident** (including date, time and whereabouts) in which you feel you have been treated unfairly. This will help you be able to recount the problem rationally, without being swept up in drama, emotions or exaggeration.

- **Tell your parents or a trusted adult.** They can then contact the school and help fix this for you. If you are already an adult, take your notes from point two to a head of department or manager to discuss the problem further. They should be able to start the ball rolling on discussing the problem with the teacher and finding a resolution.

GOODIES. Just as with friends, sometimes you will find educators who you really like and you can tell really care about you. I had an English teacher called Mrs Edge who was a total dear. She was so encouraging to work with, I felt so engaged in my lessons with her and I felt like she truly cared about my well-being. If you have teachers like this, and I'm sure you do, make sure you let them know how much you appreciate them. Like I said earlier, they're people, not robots, and just as you like to know if someone is pleased with you or if you're doing well, they do too. So, Mrs Edge, this chapter is for you. YEAH!!!

Excellent Work!

Oooooeeeeeeee, that's a lot to read and think about there! It took me a long time to write this chapter and I hope so much that it has helped you in some way.

Remember earlier when I said there were two things worth thinking about, the words 'learn' and 'success'? Think about them hard. **Your educational years are there to teach you all you need to know to be successful in the world**, but never forget that your learning is never, ever over. You learn new things every single day and success is whatever you want it to be. If success to you is being a CEO of a big-ass corporation, then go for it, but if success to you is living on a farm and caring for your collection of award-winning chickens, go for that too.

Never stop learning and never stop working towards your own version of success. ♡

Success is
whatever
you want
it to be.

BULLYING

Bullying. A mean old thing that doesn't really deserve a whole chapter. You do though. And if you are being bullied or have ever been bullied, or perhaps even are a bully, this chapter is for you.

Bullying is where a person or group of people deliberately make you feel rubbish, either verbally or physically, or both. This often happens in schools, but can also occur in non-school friendship groups, at work or in social settings. It's very cruel and can be stopped. In this chapter, we are going to talk about my own experience with bullies, why people bully and what we can do to cope with and stop the situation. Buckle up kids; this is going to be brutal.

I have been on both sides of the bullying experience – I was bullied at school by a group of very nasty girls in my class and, much as I hate to admit it, I actually was a bully to a girl in my form.

Let's start with the school bullies.

Bullies in schools are not uncommon. My bullies were a group of four girls who I think must have been deeply insecure themselves. It's tempting to name and shame them as a great act of revenge, but somehow that seems petty. They started off as my friends, but they would say mean things and, if I took offence, they would tell me 'it was a joke'. They'd criticise the things I did and excluded me from all the girlie gossip they chattered about in breaks. They made me feel unwelcome during activities and began saying cruel things to my face. When I confronted them, they said I couldn't take jokes and that I was imagining everything. I stopped being friends with them but, since we were all in the same class, I was still bothered by them. Compared to a lot of other stories of bullying, I don't think this is a particularly severe case, but when you're in the midst of it, it's hard to see the wood for the trees and it's hard to know what's the best thing to do.

During this time, I was a bully. It's upsetting to write that, because I'd like to be able to say, 'I'd never bully anyone!' But the fact is I have. There was a girl in our class who was a year younger than us, but very bright and so had moved up a form. She was polite and pleasant and kept to herself. The mean girls I was 'friends' with were horrid to her. They called her names and mocked her. In a really pathetic attempt to fit in with them, I said those cruel things too and laughed at her when I didn't need to. She must've hated those girls as much as I did but instead of standing with her, I stood against her. After I'd left the school for sixth form (I needed a fresh start away from those girls), I saw this girl at a party and apologised. She said she didn't care, but I did. I still do really.

Bullies are cowards. They spout mean things and take unkind actions because that's what they are full of, negativity. The problem with bullying is that it doesn't go away when the bullies do. It can stay with you like the smell of smoke on clothes. It lingers in your heart and makes you angry or afraid. I am still both of those things, but only in whispers. I'm angry that bullying happens and afraid that not enough people know how to deal with it and its effects.

Here are some things I did to conquer my bullies. I hope you don't ever need to use these but, if you do, I hope so much that they help.

UNDERSTAND THAT BEING BULLIED IS NOT YOUR FAULT.

No matter what the bullies say to you, it is not your fault that it is happening. The fault is entirely with the bully, who deliberately chooses to behave this way and to take these actions. They are to be pitied for making such poor choices.

BULLIES' HEARTS HURT.

For whatever reason, most bullies are struggling. They are consumed by tremendous degrees of anger, or frustration, or misery, and to try and regain some control or to feel better or to release their emotions, they bully others. Of course this doesn't make what they do alright, but it's worth considering that inside, their hearts hurt.

BULLIES ARE LIARS.

Most bullies operate on the premise that you fear them or what they say. From experience, bullies tell lies. They say things to hurt you and, to find hurtful things to say, they often need to lie. By instilling that insecurity in you, they think they have control. If you can recognise the lies (usually they are the insults), you have taken away a little bit of their control and are a step closer to freedom from them.

BULLIES FEAR CAPTURE.

I know when I was laughing at that poor girl in my class, I was always afraid that she would tell a teacher or her mother. With that knowledge, tell people! If you are being bullied, speak up. Tell teachers and parents and friends. If you are nervous, there are a lot of anonymous helplines or email services you can turn to for advice on who to tell and how to tell them. I spent a lot of time talking anonymously to the Samaritans via email and found them caring and helpful.

ONLINE BULLYING IS REAL. I think it's easy to assume that 'sticks and stones can break my bones but words can never hurt me', but this simply isn't true. With the rise of smart phones and social media platforms, there has been a rise in online bullying. Someone doesn't need to be hit or punched to be hurt; reading nasty things can be just as painful, if not more so. If you are being bullied online, there is a fair bit you can do to stamp it out.

Report the user. Every social media site has a report option. Flag up to the administrators that the user is being a bully and let the site deal with them. Usually they will be warned or have their account removed.

Block and delete. Fairly simple, just remove that person's voice from your online world and block them. With no voice, they have no power.

Save the evidence. If the bullying is persistent, screen-grab everything and write down what is being said and the dates and times of it happening. If it continues, you could have a case to take to the police. Harassment of any kind (including online) is illegal and can be dealt with by the authorities.

If I could go back to those days and relive them (which I don't think I'd really like to do, haha!), I'd do a few things differently. I'd remind myself that bullies are not worth more than me and that I am not worthless. I'd tell more people sooner about the people who bullied me and I'd accept that protecting them will not make them stop hurting me. I would be kinder to myself in every way. I'd tell myself I didn't deserve to be bullied, and that I am a nice person with a good heart, and that the bullies are sad, angry individuals.

I think I'm going to keep this chapter extra-short because it is such an un-glitzy topic and makes me feel a bit sad. If you are being bullied, I hope some of the tips I have given you from my personal experience have helped. I would also suggest you look online and ask friends, family, teachers or co-workers for their help too. The more support the better. Nobody deserves to be bullied. You are never alone and there are people that want to help and love you.

YOU ARE NEVER ALONE, THERE ARE PEOPLE THAT WANT TO HELP AND LOVE YOU.

ONLINE SAFETY

The more I think about it, the more I can't imagine
my life without the internet. 'What's the wifi password,
please?' rolls off my tongue with no thought at all,
and 'Just google it' has become second nature.
I do remember life before broadband, I even remember
life before dial-up, but it's not a way of living I ever
want to go back to.

I use the internet hard. It's my lifeline. I use it to
keep in touch with friends who are near and far, to
find things out, to watch films and programmes, to
binge on YouTube videos and, of course, to do my job.
Without it, I'd be lost – and I'm not just referring to
maps and directions!

Naturally, as with anything in life, there is a flip side to this digital playground of delights that is darker, and in this chapter we're going to look at a few ways we can keep ourselves safe online. That might sound all terribly sensible but, trust me, these tips are worth knowing.

Before we delve into how we can stay safe, we must first look at the places we might find potential danger. To find the danger, we should look at exactly what we do online. Since I don't know what eeevvvverryone does, I'll base this next bit on my own digital habits.

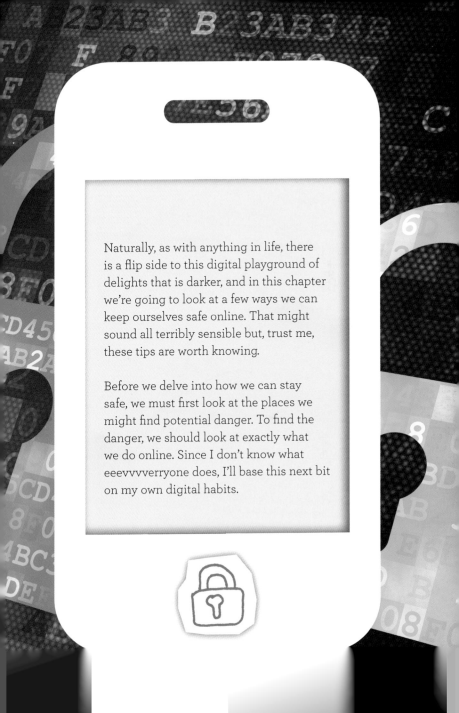

Social media for work

I am a self-confessed social media addict. My main gig is to make **YouTube** videos, and to help share them I turn to platforms like **Twitter**, **Facebook**, **Tumblr**, **Pinterest** and **Instagram**. All of my accounts on these channels have been created with the sole purpose of supporting my videos, and whilst I enjoy sharing bits of my life and being a bit silly on them sometimes, they are primarily a work tool. I try to bear this in mind at all times and keep things fairly family-friendly by limiting swear words and behaving on them how I would at a work party (do you remember that chapter?). So, I have a lot of fun with them, I am personable and approachable, I chat freely with other people but, ultimately, I don't give every little Louise-y thing out on them and nor should you.

If you are using a social media platform as a tool for work, keep it that way. Firstly, for yourself, but also for your boss/business. If you need a separate account for your drunken, undying affirmations of love to everyone you went to school with or a place to vent about waking up late, stepping on the cat and missing your bus, make one. I have an entirely personal Facebook account that is full of all the stuff I want to tell my nearest and dearest, and a lot of it would never in a thousand years make it to a Sprinkle of Glitter channel. I think I would die of cringing, haha!

Remember, you're not going to look at all cool to your manager or potential/existing customers and clients if at 2am you tweeted about eating ice cream in your ex-boyfriend's old pyjamas. Unless of course you're in the ice cream business, in which case, hit me up! What I'm trying to say here is always be mindful of keeping a professional tone online, just as you would at your actual place of work. **Just because it's online, doesn't mean it's hidden or doesn't count – it absolutely does.**

Ooooeeeee, that felt like I was almost telling you off! I wasn't, I've just learnt that lesson the hard way. Even though my job is all about being relaxed and being myself online, I still follow this rule.

Another thing you should be aware of is the people you are interacting with. Obviously, I'm not saying you need to vet every single one, but if you are starting to interact a little bit more with one person, a quick internet search on them wouldn't go amiss.

If at any point you feel worried or alarmed, all social media platforms have a report button that allows you to highlight negative behaviours or people who are being inappropriate. Take a few minutes to look out for those features and familiarise yourself with them, in case you ever have a need to use those facilities. Sounds a bit geeky, but you might one day be pleased you did it.

Shopping

Oh my, how I love internet shopping. ASOS is a place I've spent far too much of my time and Accessorize is just an oasis for me on a busy work day. I take great pleasure in perusing the pages and searching for things I really like the look of. Sometimes I play a little game with myself – I let myself have a wish basket and I fill it up with every single thing I want from the site, with no limits or restrictions. (How incredibly wild am I!) Obviously, I never purchase the basket but the fun is in the searching and finding, not so much in the having. Does anyone else do that or should I rethink my idea of a good night in?

When you are actually making a purchase, though, you are involving yourself in a financial arrangement, and that is something you should keep in mind.

 Top tip: If you are using PayPal or internet banking, always be sure to regularly change your passwords, never share them with anyone and make sure you log out every time you are done with the site. Don't just click the cross in the right- or left-hand corner, but fully log out of your online account. Doing these things will help you reduce the chance of those naughty money burglars breaking into your account.

Another little habit I have that might be worth sharing is to take a screen grab of your order confirmation page. Pretty much all retailers will send you a confirmation email, BUT just in case they don't or just in case you somehow lose it, having a screen grab will stand you in good stead if your delivery doesn't arrive, or if you need to contact the store for some reason. Once your order is safely in your sticky paws, you can just delete it, but as the old saying goes, 'It's better to be safe than sorry.'

 # Research

The internet is a crazy amazing tool for finding stuff out. If there is anything you want to know, Google (or Bing, as my little pal Eve would insist) is your friend. From train times to homework help, to recipes to Wikipedia-ing your favourite film, there is endless information out there to satisfy your thirst for knowledge.

One thing that I would say is important is to be careful about clicking on things that look really dodgy. If a site looks like something you shouldn't be on, trust your instinct and curb your curiosity. If you need to, report it to the authorities.

Yikes. Serious stuff there. Hope you don't mind!

Leisure/ watching content

Watching content on my laptop is something I actually do more than watching my TV. In fact, I could easily not own a TV and not feel like I was missing out. With the likes of **YouTube**, **Netflix**, **On Demand** and **iPlayer**, I feel downright spoilt for choice when it comes to finding something to watch for a couple of hours.

Since you aren't really interacting and are mostly just viewing, I'm not sure there is a huge deal of danger here. Mostly, I would say **change passwords often** (especially to paid prescriptions that have your financial details) and be careful what you search for. I have been known to start off looking for a beauty product review and have ended up (forty-five happy but wasteful minutes later) watching people tell their shocked kids they are going to Disney World. It's easy to get distracted and waste time on the internet, and it can interfere with your productivity! Not great if you need to be getting things done.

I think another really common online leisure activity is gaming. This is something I have never tried (do I live under a rock perhaps?), but as with everything, change passwords regularly, stick to games that are age appropriate (don't be a minx and lie about your age on the landing page, the restrictions are there for your own benefit) and do not give away personal information to other gamers you are playing and interacting with. A stranger is a stranger, even if they do love *The Sims* as much as you do. Wait, can you even play *The Sims* with strangers? See, not a gamer!

Banking

Banking is a biggie. Bank websites are like Fort Knox when it comes to security and I for one am glad they are. Many banks issue you with a magic little fob thing that I won't even try to explain the mechanics of, but what I will say is that it makes me feel really secure.

You often have to use a customer login number, password, your fobbymajoggy and then you're in! **Never write down any of your codes or details, never share them with anyone and always, always log out afterwards.**

You should treat online banking really seriously – you wouldn't saunter into a real life physical bank and shout out your PIN (I mean, please don't, it's not a brilliant idea!). So make sure you don't do the equivalent online. You want to keep all your pennies safe and sound, and where they belong!

Uploading
video
content

Oh hey there uploading content, my most favourite thing to do! Oh how I love thee.

Putting videos on YouTube is the thing I do most. Or at least I should do, but I keep getting sidetracked with other projects, like amazing books that give you tips about online safety. Heh heh.

I've been doing it for some years now and have grown a fairly substantial audience as a result. To make sure I stay as safe as possible, I abide by a few sensible rules:

▶ Avoid sharing images or footage of the front of your home.

▶ Do not share super-personal things like your National Insurance number, phone number and address. I know that seems really obvious, but you'd be amazed how often people have tripped up here.

▶ Take a little while to decide if you want to share your surname. Mine is out in the open, but I know a lot of people who prefer to keep it under wraps and I completely respect that.

▶ If you have a large following, do not give away where you are going to be at specific times. By all means tweet about the delicious dinner you just had, but maybe do that when you are home. I don't always follow this rule, but I think I probably should. I try to never say exactly where I am.

Whatever you decide to do by way of giving information out on the internet, just be aware that once it's out there, you can't take it back. Be sensible in your choices and take time to really think them through.

Connecting with friends

Using the web to connect with friends has been perfect for me and my lifestyle. I make a lot of friends through my job being a Vlogger, which means pretty much none of them live locally and so physically seeing them is rare or tricky. Tools like **Skype**, **Facetime**, **Facebook Chat** and **Twitter** are my links to keeping in touch with them and maintaining fun friendships. In fact one of my best friends, Marie, lives in Seattle and I've only ever spent a couple of weeks with her, but because we Skype every day, I feel like she is the friend I keep up to date with most! It's a crazy world we live in!

It is so important that you always know who you are talking to. If someone you don't know requests a 'friendship' online, think carefully before you accept them. Are they someone you've met before? Are they a friend of a friend or are they a complete stranger? If the answer is the latter, be savvy. Why do they want to be your friend? Could they have a sinister motive? Are they 100 per cent the person they claim they are in their profile picture?

There have been a zillion cases of people accepting these kinds of requests and building relationships (platonic or otherwise) with someone, only to discover the person behind the screen is not who they thought it was. Don't be caught out by this! If you build a friendship with someone online, make sure that you know for certain that they are who they say they are. And if at any point you begin to feel wary or afraid, speak out. Tell friends and family. If you feel like someone's behaviour towards you is inappropriate, report them to the site. If it is really very inappropriate or you feel in danger, report them to the police. Keep a diary of any incidents and screen-grab EVERYTHING. The more evidence you have, the stronger your case is.

All of the above is 'worst-case scenario' stuff, but I think it's worth knowing and having a backup plan, just in case. You should always have these things at the back of your mind when you're connecting with people on the internet.

BLOGGING

Blogging is my baby. I have been blogging since 2009 and I've been reading other people's blogs since long before that. I find it completely therapeutic to tip tap away on my laptop, writing a blog post about all the little bits of life I want to celebrate. It's cathartic – a moment where you can sit down and pour your heart out. It's a time when you can really reflect on your life and all the good things about it. My blog has been my very happy place for a long, long time and over those years I've picked up a few little ways to keep it a safe place too.

Firstly, it's important to remember that when you publish a post, anybody anywhere can see it. Don't post pictures that might put you or your family in danger. For example, if you have children or siblings, I wouldn't upload pictures of them in their school uniform because this tells strangers where the littles are during the day when you're not there. I'm not suggesting you think the worst of everything but yanno, be vigilant. The same as uploading video content really.

I know some people who prefer to blog about super-personal things, using a fake name to remain anonymous. I think that's a pretty cool idea too.

EMAILS

Ever get those emails that tell you you've won £3.4 million, and that all you need to do is send £50 to a man called Alex? Ever get those emails from the far-off-land Queen who wants to share her wealth with you, but please could you send $130 to the address below first? Ever get those emails that tell you your internet banking is down so just please give every single piece of financial information away and it will be fixed in no time?

 All. Of. Those. Are. Scams.

NEVER do them.

You will not receive your £3.4 million, nor will the Queen keep up her end of the deal, and your bank is not broken. They are just a few of the billion squillion internet scams out there, designed to make your day really extra rubbish, and it's possible for them to do you some major damage if you engage.

Hand on heart, I would say the internet's a really friendly, positive and lovely place. I very rarely have any issues, but I feel much safer in the knowledge that if there was a bit of trouble, I would know how to handle it. My hope is that this chapter has given you a couple of tips so that if something did ever pop up, you would be like a stealthy ninja and deal with it right way! Be aware and don't be afraid to talk to someone who's close to you if you have any problems online.

Enjoy the internet, use it sensibly, respect the dangers and have a great time.

Also, whilst you're on there, subscribe to my channels please! ;-)

BODY CONFIDENCE

Oh me oh my, body confidence! This is one of the chapters I've been most looking forward to writing and it's a topic I have a lot to say about. I want to share with you my own journey towards feeling like the lovely woman I deserve to be and am, and also I want to share some practical tips to help you feel that way if you don't already. If you do, please consider tweeting me (@Sprinkleofglitr) with your ideas so that we can share them with other people and spread the love.

I believe that every single baby is born perfect. When a mama holds her sweet bundle, she doesn't look down on his or her tiny body and think, 'Ew, she's a bit podgy' or 'Oh dear, he doesn't have perfect skin'. They look upon their babies with infinite love and rightfully think that they're wonderful. As we grow, we pick up insecurities and worries, and we start to feel a lot less than the incredible creatures our mothers

cradled and begin to wonder if we're good enough. We look at our friends and decide they are better, or prettier, or slimmer, or taller, or we are influenced by the media to expect a certain degree of perfection and to apply that expectation to ourselves. It's tough out there. Life can get a gal or guy down and it can be difficult to pull yourself up again.

To start you off on this chapter, I'll begin with my own experiences. Sadly, I don't think I am alone in having spent a good portion of my growing years feeling inadequate in a variety of ways. It all began when I was four years old and a little girl at school named Jodie had the most beautiful long blonde hair, with a centre parting. I, on the other hand, courtesy of my grandma's scissors and bowl-shaped kitchen-salon stylings, had Lego hair. You know the kind. The style that looks like someone has literally just plonked a chunk of hair all over your head. Thick-fringe, conker-brown, blunt-cut-just-above-the-shoulders Lego hair. I looked upon Jodie's Rapunzel-esque locks in awe and begged my mother to let me have long, non-fringed, non-Lego-like hair. 'No' was the answer – it wasn't 'practical'.

For most of lower school I lusted after long blonde locks (fast forward twenty years and rather fittingly I'm writing this paragraph in my local hair salon, as the very talented Alicia blow dries my now long and blonde hair into a dreamy princess style – childhood wishes do come true!) and felt that my practical conker Lego hair was less than enough. It was Eleanor Roosevelt who said, **'Comparison is the thief of all joy'**, and she was right.

Hair envy aside, it wasn't until I hit my teenage years that I really began to develop a lack of body confidence. At that time in your life your body is doing all kinds of crazy things. Boobs, hips, stretch marks and new hair – you're essentially a ticking time bomb of hormone-related mood swings and that can be a very frustrating path to walk down.

By the age of fourteen I was the gal with big round spectacles, a gap between my two front teeth, freckles, and a fair bit of tummy and thigh squidge, and the infamous Lego hair had evolved to something equally rubbish – wavy frizz. Honestly, I looked like a shorter, fatter, brunette Einstein. If I think about it rationally, there was nothing wrong with me at all. I still have hair frizz (which I've learnt how to tame) and I still wear glasses and I'm fine, but when you're walking through your teenage journey, a few very standard physical 'imperfections' are all that's needed to make you feel downright miserable.

As time went on, I gained more weight ('puppy fat', my auntie lovingly called it), grew my hair out (but still hadn't mastered the art of straightening it) and started to be teased by a group of really nasty girls in my class. Body confidence was at an all-time low. I really, truly thought I was physically disgusting.

Looking back, the following story is actually completely ridiculous and hilarious, but as you can imagine, at the time it was soul-destroying.

I was fifteen and at home in my suburban house in Northamptonshire. I was in my room on my computer and my dad was in the room below, which was his office. All of a sudden, out of nowhere, the walls of the house vibrated, wardrobe doors bashed about and then, as quickly as it came, it was still and silent again. Before I could process what had happened, my dad ran upstairs and in a fluster, asked if I was OK.

'Yes,' I said. 'What was that?!?!'

'I don't know!' Dad exclaimed, 'I thought you'd fallen out of bed.'

Oh. My dad had actually thought that the force of me falling 40cm out of bed would rock the entire building. Later on, the news reported that Northampton had experienced a freak earthquake. Thanks Dad. Thanks very, very much.

I carried on at school, listening to people make snide remarks about my glasses, teeth, freckles, hair or weight, and felt endlessly sad. Since the teasing was ongoing, I was never really able to pick myself up and regroup, so when it was time to decide what A-levels to do, I chose to leave and attend a sixth form college elsewhere.

By this point in my life, my dad had divorced a particularly unpleasant woman who had only added to my low body confidence and there was a definite aura of 'fresh starts'.

I started to work out which clothes suited my figure (those pale pink capri pants and strappy crop tops were not the way forward) and I began to play with new hair styles and enjoy my glasses. I started to feel alright. I looked at myself and didn't see a gross teenager (which I should never have seen in the first place), but saw bright green eyes and clear skin with beautiful freckles, thick hair that could (just about) be tamed and lovely hourglass curves.

At eighteen I left to go to university in Liverpool and felt like a new girl. In my two years at sixth form I'd made new friends and my confidence in all areas (not just my body) had blossomed. I was fine. Yes, I still had the squidgy bits and the glasses (although I also had the option of contact lenses) and crazy hair, but I had learnt to accept them and own it.

University was an absolute blast! I made a zillion (roughly) friends, loved my course and was never short of boys to go out with. I was starting to feel really happy in myself and the little push that tipped me over the edge was a comment from my friend Faye. We were in a clothing store changing room and as I turned to the side, Faye said, 'You've got such a pretty profile.' I don't know what it was about that compliment but it really struck me. I'd never allowed myself to think I was pretty. I'd heard it from uni boys in bars but brushed that off with a big dose of, 'They say that to every girl they want to chat up', but to hear it from my friend, so casually and sincerely, with no motive or agenda – it really touched me. I've never told Faye this, but really, I think that was the tipping point down the road to feeling body confident for me.

From then on, I started to just accept my not-so-great bits and focus on the parts of myself that I liked. **I started to learn little tricks and techniques to feeling good, and so I'd like to take a moment to share them with you.** It would bring me such joy to know you have read them and taken something from them because if I can be your Faye in the changing room, for me this book is a success.

TOP TIPS FOR ACHIEVING BODY CONFIDENCE

Accept.

It's very easy to look at our own bodies and be
our own worst critic. We see a little bit of wibble and
decide it's the worst, largest fat roll, or on the other side
of the coin, you might look at your legs and think they are so
slim that they look like twigs. Neither of these things is true. I
can 99.999 per cent guarantee that nobody reading this book has
the worst, largest fat roll or twigs for legs. The first step to being
body confident is simply accepting what you are, good *and* bad.
When I look at myself, I see a regular woman. I have long legs with
a bit of cellulite on my thighs. My stomach is my least favourite
part of my body, which I continue to blame on pregnancy, but if
I'm being honest with myself, it's always been a bit jibbly and
I do have the power to tone it if I choose to. My boobies,
neck and arms are all things I'm reasonably fine and
happy with, and the things I like a lot are my
cinched-in waist, my face, hair and bottom.

It's alright to have areas you like the most. We live in a culture where people are rarely encouraged to compliment themselves or point out their positive attributes. This is often misunderstood and called bragging, but yet it seems perfectly OK to say, 'Oh my tummy is so gross', etc.

At some point today, **take a moment to accept yourself** and be realistic about it. Your legs do not look like twigs, you are not the size of a whale and you absolutely don't have a pizza face. Look in the mirror and say, 'I am Louise (use your name though, otherwise things are about to get all kinds of weird). I have untoned areas but my curves are gorgeous. I have pretty lips and a sweet nose. I like my bottom. I accept that my hips are wide.'

Be very honest. Do not use damaging negative or comparative words. You are simply a human, with human parts, doing human things. Accept it.

Rationalise.

We tear ourselves apart by putting ourselves down and telling ourselves that we aren't good enough or that parts of our bodies are disgusting. We lose all sense of rationality in the process. The number of times I have heard myself angrily exclaim 'Grrr I look sooooo fat in these jeans!!!' is ridiculous, because if I were to just be totally realistic and rational, I would say: 'I look like a size 18 in these size 18 jeans', which is not 'sooooo fat'. Even though deep down we know the absolute truth about ourselves, we take things to extremes and, with that, we chip away at our self-esteem.

The trick to learn here is just a matter of self-discipline. Next time you look at a part of your body and say it's so this or so that, remind yourself that it's just a bit of body. Just slabs of fleshy meat with bones and muscles in. The same slabs of meat that seven billion other people on the planet have too. Do you think you are the only person out of seven billion who thinks they are too short/tall/fat/thin/lumpy/bumpy/kerplumpy? Nope. You are joined by the masses. Take comfort in the fact that you are not alone in your stresses and that they are only created by you. You have the absolute power to choose not to feel them.

Sometimes, before I go on stage for a show or a Q&A, I have a quick panic that since people are sat in an audience, they are going to take photographs from an unflattering angle. I envisage hundreds of shots of my double chin being splashed all over Instagram and feel a wave of distress wash over me. Then I remind myself, it's just a chin. It's just a little bit of skin on my face. I'm not the only person on the planet (or even in the room) who has a double chin. Nobody is going to look at me in horror, nobody cares except me. As soon as I remember that, I just don't care. It's not worth my time or energy, and thoughts like that are not worth yours either.

Be strong, be rational and see your body for what it is. Just a body. A body like everyone else's.

Compare. Honestly.

It's incredibly natural to look at other people and compare your body to theirs. My best friend is a petite bombshell beauty and there have been plenty of times when I've looked at her and thought, 'Oh my goodness, I wish I could have tiny features like hers or be able to pull off the type of clothes she can.' What's interesting though is that she has told me that she's on occasion looked at me and felt the same way. Once I wore a crop top with a high-waisted skirt and felt like I'd conquered Everest. Once she wore shorts without worrying and she felt on top of the world.

The point I'm trying to make is that no matter what kind of body you have, you will always look at aspects of other people and wish you had something like that. It's natural. The crucial thing to remember, though, is the old saying, 'The grass is always greener', which means you might think something else is miles better, but actually, it's no better than what you already have.

Try super-hard to spend a little less time looking at what everyone else has that you think is good, and focusing on your own positives. I promise you'll be a whole heap happier for it!

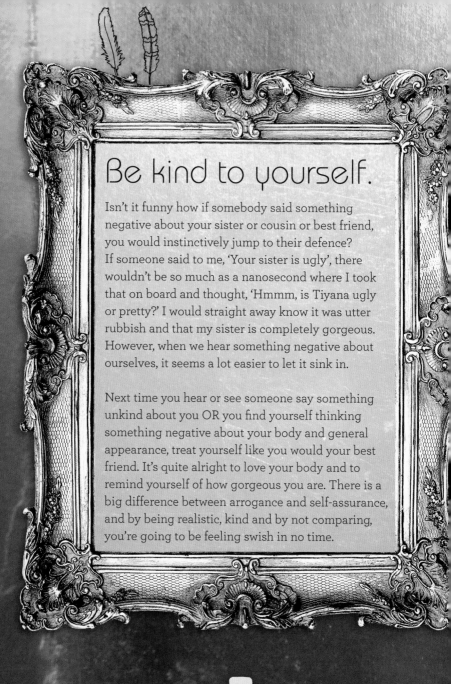

Be kind to yourself.

Isn't it funny how if somebody said something negative about your sister or cousin or best friend, you would instinctively jump to their defence? If someone said to me, 'Your sister is ugly', there wouldn't be so much as a nanosecond where I took that on board and thought, 'Hmmm, is Tiyana ugly or pretty?' I would straight away know it was utter rubbish and that my sister is completely gorgeous. However, when we hear something negative about ourselves, it seems a lot easier to let it sink in.

Next time you hear or see someone say something unkind about you OR you find yourself thinking something negative about your body and general appearance, treat yourself like you would your best friend. It's quite alright to love your body and to remind yourself of how gorgeous you are. There is a big difference between arrogance and self-assurance, and by being realistic, kind and by not comparing, you're going to be feeling swish in no time.

LOVE YOUR BODY, remind yourself how GORGEOUS you are.

Find your best bits.

Now that we've spent a little (actually a lottle!) time talking about how to handle the parts of our bodies that we feel anxious or insecure about, it's time to do a full circle and discuss the best bits! Yippee!

As I mentioned before, we live in a world where it seems almost unfashionable to talk about the parts of ourselves that we love. It's so rare that you hear a girlfriend talking about how great she thinks her legs look in that dress, instead of how big it makes her hips look or something equally negative. Buuuutttt, just because it's rare doesn't mean you shouldn't do it. You don't need to stand on stage and shout about how volumised your hair looks today (unless you want to), but you can just know it. You can know you look smokin' in whatever you are wearing and have a secret pep in your step for it.

Take some valuable quiet time to look in a mirror, click through digital pictures of yourself or just think about your body and decide what you like about it. If you have a pen and paper to hand (or technology with list-making apps), jot down all the things you think are pretty great about you. Make that list as long as you like, it's only for you so go wild! I once made a video where I asked everyone in the comments to list five things they loved about themselves and it was such a fun activity.

It's OK to love yourself. It does not make you arrogant or cocky. It makes you smart.

Flaunt it!

If you've got something you love, be proud of it. If you like your legs, wear skirts. If you have a wonderful waist, cinch it with a sweet belt. If you love your locks, go wild with headbands. You get the idea. There is no shame in being proud of your assets and making the absolute best of them.

You are allowed to like and love yourself. You are allowed to feel good and you are allowed to disagree with other people who tear you down. There is no authority on what is or isn't beautiful, we are all our own judges. **So, if you decide you look gorgeous, then you do.** Simple as that.

I hope that in reading this chapter you are reminded of how perfect you are, just the way you are.

As I said at the very beginning, we are all born that way, each and every one of us.

COMFORT ZONES

Comfort zones are a tricky old thing. At their best, you don't see them or even realise they are encircling you; at their worst, you acutely feel their absence and desperately wish to dive back into their warm, cosy embrace. Some people feel a great rush of excitement in leaving their comfort zones and some, like me, would like to spend a lifetime within their safe confines.

Of course, comfort zones are entirely invisible, specific to each individual and can shrink and swell at any time, for any reason, but we all have them. We all have places or situations or people that make us feel relaxed and safe, and activities that set us on edge and heighten our senses. Some people enjoy that sensation and some don't.

In this chapter, I'm going to talk to you about my own experiences with comfort zones and what happened when I stepped out of them. Then you can make your mind up about what you do with yours. You might even surprise yourself!

For those of you who may be unaware, a comfort zone is that intangible place where you feel safe, relaxed and unchallenged. It might be a geographical location, it might be a group of people or it might be a genre of activity. So, for example, if I was asked to cook a four-course meal, I would be completely out of my comfort zone because I am a terrible chef and have no idea what I would put together. If I was asked to make a YouTube video, I would be totally in my comfort zone, since this is a thing I do regularly and is something I don't need to really stretch myself to do. Make sense? I'll carry on.

As my life has meandered on through the years, my comfort zones have ebbed and flowed and shifted, and so has my ability to deal with them.

My biggest issues with comfort zones arise when I'm away from home. I think it's safe to say that my house is my favourite comfort zone and, if I had a choice, I'd spend all my days in it, on the sofa in fluffy PJs, working my way through a box of Cadbury's Heroes and watching Christmas movies with Darcy (even in July). As it happens, I have a job and a life and sometimes do things other than sofa/PJs/chocolates, and I have to deal with those events. For the most part, I enjoy them and have a jolly old time running errands or attending meetings, but every once in a while, mainly when I'm far away, a little panic sets in.

To make it as easy as possible for you to understand what I mean, I'm going to describe exactly how I feel. For some of you this might be super-relatable but, if not, try to empathise.

I travel a lot for work, often leaving the country to attend conventions or perform in shows, and this entails plane trips, hotels and new environments. I start off fine, excited even. I pack my suitcase and carry-on bag, load up on magazines and snacks, and feel ready to take on the world. I almost always travel with someone from my management team or another YouTuber, so I'm always in good company. Everything is fine. And then it hits. Usually once we've arrived at an unfamiliar airport or a new hotel. I suddenly feel very, very far away from home and the things that make me feel OK. I notice that everything is different. Shops aren't the same, sign posts look weird, and nothing on the TV is like I'm used to. I feel isolated and unable to tell people how uneasy I feel. I start to think I might be unwell and might throw up, and so the thought of eating makes me even more uneasy. Then I remember we all agreed to go down to dinner together and I worry about that. Will I like the food? Will it make me feel more unwell? If I need to leave, will I be able to find my way back in this unfamiliar area? Do I have enough money? (I can never work out foreign currencies well!) All these questions rattle around in my brain and I think about how much I would like to be back in my usual places, like home or the office. And then I think about how familiar everything is there.

Ultimately, I know when I'm away things are fine. I'm never going anywhere particularly adventurous and always stay in lovely places, so realistically I have nothing to fret over. Rationally, I know I will find my way back or that I could ask for directions, I know I have enough money plus my emergency credit card and I know I will like some of the food and, if I'm poorly, I know (from experience) that my friends will look after me. I just feel out of my comfort zone. And sometimes, when I'm out of it, my brain goes on a bit of a holiday and I can't seem to make sensible thoughts happen. I need a little bit of help. I'll give you a real life example.

A few months ago, I flew over to New Jersey to attend a convention for YouTubers. I flew out with my friends Jack and Dean, but was nervous because it was an area of America I'd never been to before and the people I usually go to these things with (like my manager, Maddie, or Zoe and Alfie) weren't going. I decided not to limit myself and go anyway because I'm close with Jack and knew he'd 'get it' if I didn't do very well. I think if you are a person who struggles with comfort zones, it's important to have someone who understands. When you're in the midst of dealing with an issue, you really don't want to have to try and explain all of that to someone. Jack got it.

We flew over and had a great flight. I gave the boys mini-facials with all my beauty bits and they entertained me with their winning humour. On arrival, I started to feel that dread in my tummy. The sense of not being able to grasp on to anything familiar and feeling a bit like things are spiralling out of my control. Luckily it was late; we got to our hotel quickly and went to bed. Jack's room was right next door to mine, so I felt comfortable knowing he was close by. When I type all this out, it sounds so silly. I just asked myself: 'Why did he need to be nearby? What was going to happen?' And the answer is, 'I don't know.' I do hope this is making sense for some of you!

The next day, a few of Jack and Dean's friends met up with us in the hotel and it was decided that we would all go into New York City to have a look around and experience it. Oh wowee. I did not feel excited about that. Instantly, my mind began to race with all the things that made me uncomfortable. Would I get lost? Would I be able to get back alone if I needed to? Would it feel overcrowded? Would they talk to me? (A stupid one, but when there's a big group of people, it's easy to be a little pushed out.) All these things whirred around in my head, and I caved in to them and said I couldn't go.

That's the annoying thing about comfort zones. They have a very strong pull and even when you want to do something, like explore New York, they whisper to you that it will be scary or that terrible things will happen and invite you to step away and stay within them, where it's 'safe'. I usually ignore this feeling and do it anyway, but on that day it was too much.

Lucky for me, Jack saw my little worry wobble and convinced me to come out with them all, promising to look after me. The day was a successful failure I think.

We took a cab into the city and the ride was alright. I chatted to some friends, but at the back of my mind I knew I was on edge. We walked a few blocks to a restaurant and, having never experienced the busy streets of New York before, it was quite a culture shock – and I've weathered Oxford Street in December! By the time we were seated at our table and the food arrived, I had relaxed and was glad I'd been dragged out of the hotel. I was feeling confident and pleased... but then we went to Times Square. I don't know if you've ever been there before but, if you haven't, the only way I can describe it is 1 million per cent sensory overload. Every which way you look there are tourists bustling past, flashing billboards, big bright screens, advertorials, people in crazy costumes, buildings taller than you can crane your neck to see. It's A LOT. And that's when it hit.

For me, the pinnacle of feeling out of my comfort zone is when I start to feel poorly. I said as calmly as possible to a lovely girl called Amber (to whom I will always be grateful for being so kind to me that day), 'I think I've got about ten minutes before I'm really unwell. I need to go to a bathroom.' We zipped over to a restaurant, I dived into the loos, threw up (sorry, TMI) and twenty minutes later sat crying on a bar stool whilst Jack handed me water and told me that everything would be OK. I really, really let being out of my comfort zone get the better of me.

After Jack had been a complete love, I did stay out. We went shopping, glided round an ice rink under twinkly lights and sipped hot chocolate. It was a perfect day. I was so glad to have had friends who helped me. I wish I had been calm enough to do that myself.

Since that successful failure though, I've been away from home a handful of times and I've always managed to stay in control. Every time I feel myself slipping into panic, I remind myself of 'the worst', which was being sick in Times Square. It was fine. I was sick. So what? Then I had a great day. I tell myself that if the very worst happens, I'll be sick and then I'll be fine. It's actually very comforting, facing your fears like this, and it allows me to feel strong and able.

So that's my absolute biggest tip for you. Face your fear. Ask yourself, 'What is the absolute worst that can happen?' And then answer it. For me, the worst that can happen is that I get lost or I am poorly. To combat that I always write down the name of the hotel in my phone and make sure I have enough reserve cash to get a taxi back at any point. And if I'm ill, well it's fine.

For me, in terms of stepping out of my comfort zone, that really was the worst-case scenario, but sometimes you can step outside of your comfort zones in much smaller ways, in your day-to-day life. So, here are some little tips that might help you to recognise those safe places, and help you step out of that comfort zone and grow as a person:

❀ **TAKE THINGS SLOWLY.** You don't need to jump in with a ten-hour day in New York City. Take baby steps and allow yourself to very gently leave your comfort zone, and then hop back in. That way, you will feel safe in your leaving and perhaps you'll feel more confident to try it again afterwards. For me, that's doing things like going out with my friend Clare when she invites me. Clare is the most social lady I know and has more friends than I can count. Sometimes she invites me to join them for dinners or parties and, although I don't know the other guests, I always try to say yes and give it a go. The girls are always so friendly and I end up really enjoying myself and feeling glad that I went. If you are invited to something you're a bit nervous of, remember my story and give it a whirl.

❋ **HAVE INCENTIVES.** When I have to try something new that I'm scared of, I think about the benefits of those things. Often it's just little things like, 'I might be able to take a couple of nice photos for Instagram' or 'Maybe they'll have some nice shops there', but whatever those small things are, they make me feel excited to go to them and often this encourages me to step out of my comfort zone. Have a think about the situation and what good could come of it, and you might feel more inclined to give it a go.

❋ **BRING COMFORTS WITH YOU.** Wherever I am, I always have my phone with me. If I'm feeling at all worried or upset, I spend a couple of seconds flicking through my pictures and thinking about all the funny memories I've shared with friends, or sweet moments I've had with Darcy. This helps me to feel relaxed and able to deal with whatever situation I'm in.

❋ **EXPLAIN HOW YOU FEEL TO FRIENDS.** I've spent quite a long time explaining my anxieties to my friends and now when I go to stay with them (since being away from home is being out of my comfort zone for me), they make such lovely efforts to help me. Hazel always tells me she's put fresh sheets on the spare bed and that I can have a whole bathroom to myself (haha) and Zoe always stocks the fridge with my favourite snacks and leaves little things on the bedside table to make me feel cosy. They are good friends! I'd suggest telling your friends about what sets you on edge and I bet they will try and help you. Equally, be a listening ear for your friends if they have things they want to talk about too.

I hate stepping out of my comfort zone. It frightens me. I have to admit though that, when I do, amazing things happen. In many ways, my whole job is a big step out of it. I used to be a quiet office worker with a simple happy life and now I have a very exciting career that takes me all over the world and brings me a lot of incredible opportunities. Often they make me scared and sometimes I try to back out of doing them but, in the end, once I've pushed through the fear, they are amazing.

That day in New York was, eventually, one of the most magical days I've ever had. As I was on the ice rink, I took a moment to look around at the skyscrapers and twinkling Christmas lights and I thought, 'I'm so lucky to be here.' If I hadn't stepped out (or been forced to, thank you, Jack) of that comfort zone, that moment would not have existed for me. My best friend Zoe has a little saying she lives by, which is 'Just say yes.' I don't always manage this, but I am trying more and more, and so to conclude this chapter I would offer you her advice too – just say yes. Who knows what adventures it might take you on!

Good luck glitterbugs!

GIVE IT A WHIRL

All about Love

Boys and Lurve   204

DATING   218

BONDING WITH BABY   230

Being Kind   240

BOYS
+
LURVE
♡

Takes a deep breath

I have been saving this chapter until now because, honestly, I'm afraid. I'm a fully grown woman afraid to talk about boys. How ridiculous!?

Boys have always been entirely intriguing to me and yet utterly bamboozling at the same time. I'm going to write this chapter as if I am talking to a little sister. I'm going to try and impart my wisdom (or what little there is of it in this field) to you in a bid to make you feel confident with those strange creatures but, ultimately, there is a good chance that you know more than I do and that you could teach me a thing or two!

My very first confusing experience with a boy was when I was four. It was my first day at lower school and whilst the teacher called the register, I noticed a sweet little boy we'll call Tom, with curly brown hair and freckles. In my naive mind, I decided he would be my friend and that we'd sit together for story time. Off I plodded and as I flumped down next to him, I said, 'I'm Louise and I think we'll be friends now.' He pushed me and told me that he hated girls and to get away.

A few years later, when I was eight, I got hitched in a playground wedding to a boy we'll call Tim, who had no bedtime and read at an age level of two years above him – what a catch! We talked a little bit about pets (I had a Russian hamster called Celeste and he had a dog called Bounty) and a little bit about a boy we'll call Toby (his 9-year-old arch nemesis, who always had a runny nose), but for the most part we actively ignored each other because members of the opposite sex were considered utterly repulsive and to be avoided at all costs.

That whole idea is mad. Why did we all think this way? We wanted to 'marry' all the boys (and they must've wanted to 'marry' us, otherwise why did they hold our hands and give us freshly picked dandelions?), and yet we wanted to run away from them and say they were gross.

Things never really cleared up for me because at the age of nine I was transferred to an all-girls school, where I stayed until I was sixteen. When I left, wowee wowee wowee, was I so confused by boys!

Rather than going through every tiny detail, I'll just recount for you the key 'boy moments' in my life. I'll save the dating horrors for the next chapter but, still, you can laugh at my expense as you see how utterly inept I was and am at being cool with boys.

THE FIRST KISS

At my all-girls high school there was a distinct shortage of boys. Unless you had a crush on the elderly biology teacher or you were into girls (in which case, you lucked out big time), there was nothing in the way of hotness for you to enjoy. Then, like Cinderella being told she's going to the ball by the Fairy Godmother, a friend of mine started attending the local boys' grammar school (they let girls in at sixth form) and it was party invite, after party invite, after party invite. I was in hormone-fuelled heaven and I liked it!

It was at one of those parties that I had my first kiss. Was it magical and full of love? No. No it fully was not.

Now, 16-year-old Louise thought she looked gorgeous. Not just OK, but drop-dead OMG, FML GORGEOUS. Looking back, I've since realised that I looked a hot mess, but it's how you feel that counts, right? It was a Halloween fancy dress bash and I'd gone for a black pencil skirt, black cami top, black tights, my friend's black heels and some red battery-operated flashing devil horns (with the battery pack not at all cleverly disguised in my hair, which for some reason I'd decided to scrape into a bun). Why didn't my best friend at the time tell me that I looked like a total div? Because she was dressed the same, only with red fishnet tights instead of regulars – she always was the more adventurous one.

So, there we are, two badly dressed but overly confident teenagers, standing alluringly at the side of the room (that is, standing at the side of the room, watching boys throw themselves around the dance floor and thinking how cool they all looked), when over swans a tall gawky boy we'll call Tristan. He asks me to sit down. We sit in awkward silence and then he kisses me. Big, all-encompassing face smooches, at a table, with batteries on my head. Mmmmmm, romantiiiiiicccccc.

The fun didn't stop there, oh no. After a while of him almost eating my actual face, he starts doing what I rather stupidly assume to be neck kisses. Big, sucky, squelchy neck kisses. Neck kisses that were actually love bites, as I found out the next morning, when I woke up at my friend's house and my dad was only twenty minutes away from collecting me. No amount of Collection 2000 concealer could hide those beauties and I had to tell my dad what had happened.

Not the most fairytale-esque first-kiss experience, but solid ground for improvement over the years!

Friends who are boys are a whole different kettle of fish (whatever that means) to gal pals. I have found it harder to have really close guy friends than girls friends, but when I do find one, I love them very, very dearly. I find that with guy friends you can be just that little bit blunter, but you absolutely have to allow them to be blunt back to you. Haha! This is something I still have trouble with. Boys, I have found, like banter – it's just a bit of light teasing, done all in jest and full of good spirits – but if you don't learn to take it well, it can be a stinger. I've definitely learnt that fact the hard way and I like to think I've toughened up and mastered the art of give and take with it. Hurrah for me! How do you fare?

If you get really lucky, though, you get the kinda guy friends I have. The kind who will look after you when you're in a tizzy before boarding a flight or the kind who will listen to you ramble on and on via Skype about all the trials and tribulations of your day. They are special people.

YOU
SHINE

Guy friends (for me at least) are not like your girls, who you can discuss periods, gossip and secrets with, but they are kind and caring and loyal and lovely. The most important boy friends in my life right now are Alfie Deyes and Jack Howard, who never (well, almost never, heh heh) fail to take care of me when I need them to and give me all the LOLs, even when they're at my expense! I hope they read this and feel oh-so-special to be in my book. *big squishy feels*

IF YOU FIND A GOOD GUY FRIEND,
TREASURE HIM.
IF YOU FIND A REALLY GOOD GUY FRIEND,
PUT HIM IN A BOOK ;)

UNREQUITED LOVE

Ohhhhhh, the very worst kind of love. The kind of love you desperately wish you could discard and that makes you tell yourself every week that it is no longer affecting you and that you are in control of it, and not the other way round. Been there, done that, got the cringe-y memories.

The object of my desire was my flatmate in my freshers' year at university. I don't know why I thought he was so cool, but 18-year-old Louise really did. He was impressively sure of himself, well travelled, could cook pasta and rode around on a blue motorbike. A teen dream. Looking back now, I know it wasn't actually 'love', but that's the sneaky thing when it's unrequited – it's so intense that you can't tell, and you just find yourself sucked into an inescapable vortex of feeeeeeeeellllings for someone who doesn't feel them back. I know because I was pretty blatant (in other words, I threw myself at him one night) and was totally and utterly rejected. Oh the pain!

It didn't take me long to get 'over' him because I met someone else a few months later, but oh my goodness gracious, it wasn't fun liking him as much as I did when he didn't like me back. Fortunately for me, he moved to the other side of the world a few years later, so although we remained friends and things weren't as dire as they were in my first year at uni, I'm still kind of glad I don't have to deal with him. I'm also very much hoping that they don't sell my book in the country he now lives in!!!

If you are in a similar situation, I have harsh advice for you: Get. Away. From. Him. Do not kid yourself that you can just will yourself out of loving them (for me it took a great big whirlwind relationship with someone else; for friends of mine it has taken never seeing them again or a big argument). Do not kid yourself either that you can do something to make him like you. You can't. The only proper way to have someone like you is for them to fall for the person you are. **Never try to alter yourself to please someone**, because eventually that act will slip and you will be in a pickle. His opinion does not define you. **You are perfect just as you are.** Take some space, walk away and fill your time and head with other, more healthy things. I promise you that after a while (the first bit will be hard, I know), you will feel so much better and clearer. Good luck!

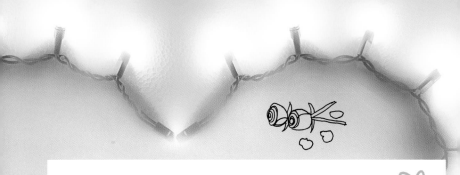

BOYFRIENDS

My first boyfriend actually turned out to be the man I married and the father of my child, so in this area I'd say I did pretty well! I met Matt through a mutual friend in September 2004 and instantly thought he was a total babe. I remember very distinctly thinking, though, 'Oh no, he's way out of my league, I'm not even going to think about him in that way.' Turns out, he thought the same about me. After a lorra lorra shillyshallying and he-said-she-saids between friends, by 1 June 2005 we had become an official item and I spent that summer drunk on love. I adored being Matt's girlfriend. I rented a studio apartment in the city (remember that I mentioned I failed seven out of ten exams in my first year of uni? Well, I had to retake them), and during the day he went to his job waiting tables in a café while I revised. Then, in the evening he'd come over and we'd eat yummy treats, watch *Lost* or go for starlit walks along the Albert Docks. It was perfect. The most dreamy, wonderful summer I think I've ever had, actually.

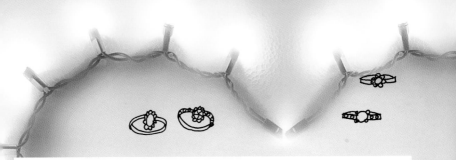

I never felt like I had to try and we didn't play games with each other. There was none of this, 'wait thirty minutes before texting back' or 'don't offer to buy the first drink on the date' rubbish. It was just two people who loved being with each other, being with each other.

If you meet someone and you click, go for it. If you meet someone and it's hard work, with a million obstacles and no chemistry, don't force it. **If love is there, like pink petals in spring, it will blossom.**

So what can we learn from all this? That I am a bumbling buffoon who needs to take a breath before she speaks or acts? That big, sloppy neck kisses don't always turn out so good? Yes, that, but also: boys are weird and they are confusing, but I bet you they think the same about us girls.

Ultimately, I think they want to be treated with respect and want to spend time with people who make them laugh or people who care about them. Try not to be like I was, and just approach boys the same way you would anyone else, with warmth and kindness and a positive attitude.

I think if I had to give my 16-year-old self five top tips for approaching boys they would be:

1. SMILE. Nothing is easier and shows that you're approachable than a smile. Also, it's actually quite hard to not return a smile, so you're already onto a winner with that one.

2. TAKE BREATHS. When I get nervous or excited (or both), I talk a lot faster, laugh harder and zip about like a bit of a maniac. If I remember to take a few breaths here and there, it gives my brain just enough time (and extra oxygen) to remind my body to caaaalllllmmmm down, and stop being such a nut. A calmer you is going to come across a lot more cool and confident.

3. HAVE A PASSION. People like people who like things. People aren't thrilled by people who don't care about anything or who have zero interest in life. Basic. The thing I never realised was that it doesn't actually matter what you're interested in, as long as there is something. If you have a deep passion for collecting vintage magazines, talk about it! If you have a great love for photographing people's pets whilst they wear fresh floral crowns (I know this person!), talk about it! It might not be his exact interest, but it's intriguing to talk to someone about theirs. It shows that you have a bit of depth to you and that's very, very attractive.

4. WHY SO SERIOUS?

Chatting to boys is not supposed to be an awful chore to endure, so relax a bit. Laugh at yourself and if you mess up, you're only human, just like him. Chances are he's a bit nervous too, so he'll probably be grateful for a little giggle at things if they're going awry.

5. BE YOURSELF.

Such a classic – an oldie but a goldie. This is the one that took me the very, very longest to grasp. I would waste so much of my energy observing 'cool girls', either in real life or on TV, and trying to emulate them. It never worked; you can't be someone you're not. Looking back, I know I would have felt a whole heap better if I had just let myself be me – I'm alright really, haha! It's a tough stance to take but if a guy (or gal), doesn't like the very real you, move on. When you find the person who does totally, ding ding ding, you've found a keeper!

WHATEVER YOU DO WITH THE OPPOSITE (OR SAME) SEX IN LIFE, RESPECT THEM AND YOURSELF, NEVER LIE, AVOID PLAYING GAMES AND, ABOVE ALL, ENJOY YOURSELF AND EACH OTHER.

DATING

Dating. The most wonderfully terrifying way to spend an evening. Ha, I jest! It's alright really. In this chapter, I'm going to let you in on my dating experiences (some great, some utterly traumatic) and, just like in all the other chapters, I'll give you some tips. I would say, though, I'm not a dating expert. In fact, I'm probably closer to 'dating disaster' than expert, but here goes!

THE FIRST DATE

Picture the scene. It was 2002 and after one of those Boys School parties I told you about in the Boys and Lurve chapter, my battered Nokia 3210 (that's what we had before iPhones) beep-beeped. The boy who I'd spent a good portion of the previous night smooching had asked me on a date. Good golly Miss Molly, the excitement!

Now, this may surprise you (ha) but 16-year-old Louise was a dweeb. Coolness did not (and still doesn't) run through my veins and, frankly, I was just amazed someone wanted to take me out. So I said yes and we agreed on a trip to the cinema.

The next week was spent with nothing but thoughts of preparing for this date. Good hair straighteners hadn't yet been invented at this point, so the odds were already against me. As was my severe lack of any fashion sense. So, I did my best and wore my black stretchy boot-cut trousers (which I also wore to my Saturday job at a local supermarket, but I thought they were smart so a good option), a pink fluffy angora high-neck jumper, hair brushed out and semi straightened with my steam irons (it looked awful, like cavewoman hair after an electrocution) and a lorra lorra baby-pink lipgloss.

I. Looked. Terrible.

I'm cringing now just thinking about it.

Despite my poor fashion choices, my dad told me I looked a million dollars, took a picture of me on the drive to preserve the memory of 'Louise's First Date' and drove me to the cinema. In the car, he droned on and on about how I was growing up, and that life was a series of steps on a path, and something about maturing. Mostly, I was just glad he didn't talk about boys or sex and that the cinema was only a fifteen-minute drive away.

I walked confidently in (years and years of reading my step-mother's *Cosmo* magazines had taught me that 'confidence was key'), spotted him in the foyer and planned to say something suave.

'You're taller than you were sitting down!' is what I did say, though. Smooth. So, so smooth.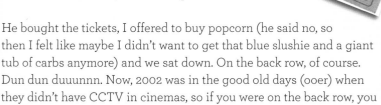

'Ha. Yeah. Errrrrr... Hi,' was his response. Nailed it.

He bought the tickets, I offered to buy popcorn (he said no, so then I felt like maybe I didn't want to get that blue slushie and a giant tub of carbs anymore) and we sat down. On the back row, of course. Dun dun duuunnn. Now, 2002 was in the good old days (ooer) when they didn't have CCTV in cinemas, so if you were on the back row, you knew there was going to be an element of smoochery. Uh oh.

Then the credits rolled and it was time to go and find my dad in the carpark. No conversations, no getting to know each other, not really a great date. But don't tell 16-year-old Louise that, because she thought it was incredible!

Some things that I learnt from this date were that black stretch trousers and pink fluffy jumpers don't do anyone any favours, and that having a first date in silence in a dark room isn't really a fabulous way to get to know someone.

Did I make that mistake again? Yes. Yes I did.

THE POO MAN DATE

Fast forward two years to 2004, and I had another crush. This time on a guy from my course at university, and this time it was big.

I spent a good portion of the academic year swooning over him and thinking that, truly, he was the bees knees. I'm trying to remember what it was about him that I liked so very, very much, but when I think about it, I really don't know. We had nothing in common and I don't remember any huge LOLs – so goodness knows what I was so excited about, but nevertheless, I was in a dither.

By the summer, he'd asked me out on a date and I was cray cray ready for it. After all, I'd spent the last eight months flitting around him, trying my best to be 'cool' and 'alluring', so a date only confirmed my success!

I'd been shopping with my friend Faye to buy a new outfit – marginally better than the black trousers/angora jumper combo. This time it was blue boot-cut jeans (hey, they were *in*), a black lace cami top and a raspberry-pink cardigan. Not really *that* bad, I don't think.

He arrived at my building with a bunch of tulips (good) and after I had schlepped back up seven flights of stairs (bad) to drop them in my flat, we were off.

Now, I don't quite know what happened but it was the opposite of a miracle. What's that called? A disaster? Whatever you call it, something went wrong. On the less than ten-minute walk from flat to cinema, I fell completely and utterly out of lust with him. In that moment, I just stopped being attracted to him, altogether. He had done nothing. He looked lovely. He'd bought flowers. But no. The magic had gone. *POOF!*

What a great time to fall out of like with someone, on the way to the date. So there we were, in the theatre, watching the film (I forget which) and all I can think is: 'I bet he's going to want to kiss me. Oh no! OH NO! I'm going to have to kiss him!' In retrospect, I wish I had considered the fact that I had a choice and didn't actually *have* to kiss anyone, but in the panicked moment, I wasn't thinking straight.

After a little while, I calmed down and convinced myself that actually I would like to kiss him (as you can see, I'm pretty fickle!) and that it would be fine. I would kiss him. I would enjoy a kiss with him. Mmmmm smoochy.

As the film ended, we walked to the doors and I thought, this is it, we'll probably kiss and then go our separate ways home. But no, all of a sudden, he turned to me and said very seriously, 'Louise, I just need to nip to the toilet – it's a big job.' A 'big job'. A poo. He needed a poo on our date. He couldn't wait fifteen minutes to get home to poop. POOP. ON A DATE.

I was aghast. I couldn't kiss a man who had just had a POO. No. Not an option. I needed a plan!

I dashed into the ladies and text him: 'Hey, Faye's having a crisis at the flat, had to rush back. See you on Monday, thanks for a lovely evening!! xx'.

Phew! I was saved! I stayed in the loos an extra twenty minutes to be on the safe side and then ventured out into the foyer. And there he was. There he was, standing waiting for me. WHAT. FRESH. HELL.

'Are you OK?' he asked.

'Errrr yes,' I replied.

We walked outside without talking and there was a beep beep. My text pinged through onto his phone. Confusion danced all over his face. WHAT FRESH HELL AGGAAAIINNN. Turns out, there was no signal in the loos, my message hadn't gone through, he'd waited for me thinking *I* was the cinema pooer and we never dated ever again. URGH.

223

THE SANDMAN DATE

Another year on and a friend of mine had convinced me to go speed dating with her. If you're unfamiliar with the concept, speed dating is where all the ladies sit at their own table and each lady is joined by a man. You talk for about five minutes, then someone rings a bell and all the men move on to the next table, with the next lady at it. Both the men and the women have a list of names of their dates, and if you like someone you've chatted to, you give them a little tick. If you both tick each other, the organiser will give you their contact details and from there you can set up a proper date. It's all fun and games. In theory.

As it happens, I had 'ticked' a guy and he'd 'ticked' me and we'd arranged – you guessed it – a cinema date. What was wrong with me?!?! As usual, looking back, I'm not sure what the appeal was but there must have been something I liked so once again I found myself throwing on clothes and overdoing the lip gloss, ready for my big night.

By this point I think I'd improved a little in the fashion stakes – the real challenge was actually getting there on time. I lived slightly further away and was a flibbertigibbet, so I ended up arriving a few minutes late and just hoped he wouldn't mind.

He did.

'Sorry I'm late! Have you been waiting long?' I garbled on arrival.

He told me very sternly he'd been waiting thirty minutes and asked if I had I got lost. Good start.

And then I noticed it. This man had turned up to the date in – and this is no word of a lie – beige loafers (they didn't have a tassel but there was an element of fringing to them, thank you please), light trousers (the 'smart casual' kind that over-35s wear to garden parties, you know), a white shirt and a cream-coloured jacket. He had blond hair and pale skin and so looked like a walking stick of butter. It was incredible. If he'd have walked past a sandy beach, he'd have been invisible.

Sandman attire aside, he whisked me through to the ticket lady, no offer of drinks or snacks in sight (I'd have bought them for us but he wasn't even stopping and, after my telling-off for being late, I daren't ask for any), and it was film time.

As with all the others, it was a flop. After a brief line about, 'I've got a lot of uni work on, I'll call you,' we were away and I never saw my sandy prince again.

'I'll call you...'

THE TAMPON MAN DATE

Around the same time as my date with the Sandman, I met an American in a bar. He was handsome and suave and my friends liked him, so I took it upon myself to flirt mercilessly with him until he was in love with me.

I'm not sure I quite got there, but he said I was cute and asked me for my number. Hurrah! A few days later, he text and invited me to his apartment for 'wine and a movie' and in a great big dither of excitement, I said yes.

As usual, I faux pas'd on the fashion front but, in my defence, green jeans were really cool in 2005. I just didn't see the memo about not pairing them with baby-pink smock tops and dangly earrings. Oh well.

I had a lot of hope for this one; it wasn't a date at the cinema after all. So there I go, skipping off to Mr America's luxury duplex apartment (that he had as well as his apartment in the Bahamas, don't you know – and he talked about that A LOT).

He offered me red wine (which I hate), and we watched *Ocean's Eleven* (which I also hate) and chatted about this and that and all things in between. It was going pretty well, I thought.

Until, he offered me a tour of his pad.

We looked around each room, and he gave thrilling commentary like: 'And here's the office. That's my computer. That's my filing cabinet. This is my work bag.' Yanno, that standard of small talk, and then we reached his bedroom. Automatically I felt weird looking at his bed, where he sleeps, where he... you know, but I remained cool and classy and said how nice the art on his walls was. Then he went into what I can only describe as the *most* detailed room tour of my life – opening wardrobe doors, showing me his suits, pointing out pictures of friends on boats in tropical locations, until finally he opened his bedside cabinet and, along with a load of other gubbins about it, he said, '...and I have some spare tampons here if you need any?'

'Errrr... no. No thank you. Why do...? Where did they...? I'm fine, thank you...'

Very, very weird.

And so I think you can see, I am no dating expert. I have of course had some pretty wonderful dates too, weekend trips in London with views from the Shard and brunch at Borough Market, pizza picnics by the Albert Docks and long walks on Formby beach. So remember, for every bad date, you're definitely owed a good'un.

If you are in the dating game, my absolute biggest tip is: just be yourself. If you're in it for the long term, there's no point pretending to be someone you're not because eventually that facade is going to slip and they'll eventually get to know the real you anyway. You may as well give yourself straight away and if they love it/can handle it (haha), then you're going in the right direction.

Be patient and kind with your date, have an open mind and remember that they might be a little bit scared or nervous too.

Above all, go into dating with a happy heart, a smile and a positive attitude and I think you will have such a lot of fun with it.

If you have any hilarious dating stories, though, please do share them with me on social media, they always tickle my pickle! Teehee!

GO INTO
DATING WITH
A HAPPY
HEART, A
SMILE AND
A POSITIVE
ATTITUDE.

For me, bonding with baby began when I was pregnant. Darcy was a planned addition to our family so I was eagerly awaiting a positive pregnancy test, and the minute I saw those faint pink lines, I started to imagine the infant I would soon hold in my arms.

Throughout the next nine months I found myself quite innately doing a lot of things that helped me bond with my future daughter. I'm glad I had the opportunity to do all of those things because they are now some of my most special memories and also made adjusting to her arrival all the easier.

Attending all my appointments and scans.

This sounds like an obvious one, but I really looked forward to each appointment because I felt a little bit closer to Darcy each time I went. I knew that what I was doing (endless blood pressure tests and injections, etc.) was for her benefit and the real treats were hearing her heartbeat thud-thud-thudding and seeing the scans of her. Seeing her small body flicker on the screen was such a wonderful moment for me. It made everything seem so real and helped me imagine her in my tummy even more vividly.

The gender reveal.

We chose to find out the sex of our baby at the 20-week scan. I'm so glad we did that, because it allowed us to prepare in advance and helped me to really imagine a life with a little girl, rather than flip-flopping between 'If it's a girl... If it's a boy...' I'm not big on surprises. I never actually said this out loud before the scan, but I really did want a little girl. I was so happy when the sonogram technician told us that I cried. Then Matt cried. Then the technician cried! All three of us were a mess of happy emotions and all the while not-yet-born Darcy flickered about on the screen, having her own little *in utero* party.

Choosing a name.

That night, we went to dinner to tell people the sex, and on the way home Matt said, 'How about "Darcy"?' We'd been playing the name game for weeks and although there was a firm list of names we liked, Darcy just seemed to click, and I knew right away that that was my daughter's name. By having a name picked out, I felt the bond with her so much more. It also felt so wonderful when she was born because the midwife said, 'She's here! Here's your Darcy!'

Preparing her room.

Whilst I was pregnant, I was made redundant from my (rubbish and boring) office job so, with just one income, money was verrrryyyyy tight. Despite that, though, I still found plenty of ways to make her bedroom special. I took little bits of decor from our wedding and displayed them on the walls (glittery white butterflies, my sparkly veil, etc.), hung photos of all our family, made a sweet mobile out of an embroidery hoop, ribbon and coloured card, painted an old bookcase white, painted the inside of the old wardrobe pink and had my lovely grandad put up some shelves for me so I could display some of her sweet things. Spending time pouring so much love into the room that would be hers really set my mind on the lovely new addition we were going to have to the family.

With our budgets being very tight, there were a lot of things we didn't have the opportunity to do or to buy, but when I look back, I don't feel like I missed out on anything at all. I made do with what I had and cherished everything all the more. Our families were so very generous (Matt's parents bought us the pram I really wanted, my Auntie Jackie bought us a beautiful bassinet and Auntie Judith hand stitched Darcy a patchwork quilt that she still snuggles) and we were so resourceful that I only look back on that period in my life with love. Babies really are a blessing.

Once Darcy was born, bonding took a little longer for me than it did Matt. I had a very difficult delivery and afterwards didn't feel myself, physically and mentally. My body healed very quickly but for a long time I felt very distressed by memories of the delivery and would often replay the traumatic parts in my mind and I'd struggle to cope. I spoke to my midwife about this a lot and she referred me to a counsellor, who was fantastic. I also had a few extra home appointments from my health visitor and would take Darcy every Tuesday to a local clinic to have her weighed (she had trouble gaining weight at the start and this was a great worry for me). All of these services were free. I know a lot of people complain about the NHS, but when I think back to how much support they offered me, I am very thankful.

The message here though is, if you are suffering, tell someone. It is very natural to struggle after giving birth, you have been through a big ordeal and although you have your sweet bundle of joy, it was probably not that fun getting them into your arms! Give yourself a break, if you feel like something isn't quite as it should be, there is no shame in telling a professional and taking the help you need. If you don't feel that instant rush of love, don't worry about it, it will come. Some people feel it straight away and others, like me, need a little more time to come to terms with what their body has been through before they can be in that head space. For a long while I felt like this meant I was deficient in some fashion or that I wasn't loving her enough. I wish someone had told me that it was alright to let love blossom and unfurl like the petals on daisies. It will come and it will be all the sweeter for the wait.

Let love blossom and unfurl like the petals on daisies.

Once Darcy hit the three-month mark she was sleeping through the night, I had our routine down to a fine art and I felt confident that I could manage. I felt my love grow more strongly for her each and every day. I had loved her the minute I knew she was in my womb, but as she grew from a newborn to a bouncy baby, I fell more and more in love with her little personality, and this is when I truly felt that unbreakable mama–baby bond.

To help nurture that, I found the following activities helped a lorra lot:

Mummy mornings.

I live in the suburbs and I found there was a myriad of classes I could attend with Darcy. A lot of them were run by the NHS or by local churches, and usually they were in community centres, and there were plenty of toys and games out for Darcy and other mums for me to chat to. As I mentioned earlier, I also really enjoyed taking her to baby clinic once a week to have her weighed, because it was an opportunity for me to talk to a health professional and have the reassurance that I was doing OK. I think if you are missing important people in your life (for me it's my own mother, who died when I was little), that gentle pat on the back from someone who knows what they're doing is really valuable. It helped me relax and just enjoy Darcy's babyhood. If you have a little one now or on the way, take a bit of time to research if there is anything like this in your area. It's so worth it.

Skin-to-skin and sensory play.

Babies cannot communicate with speech in the way we do and so a lot of their communication comes from sight, soothing sounds and touch. When Darcy was a teeny weeny, I would lay her on my chest when I had baths and just spend quiet time pouring warm water on her little hands and cooing over her. I know she loved this and studies have shown that skin-to-skin contact helps regulate a baby's heartbeat and keep their temperature constant. Unfortunately, I was only able to breastfeed for a short time (we had a lot of complications that ended in a rather upsetting week in hospital) and so by spending this time together, without screens or other people or distractions, we were allowed to just soak up each other's love and bond our hearts together. It is such a cherished memory for me.

Chatting.

The simplest thing I did to bond with Darcy was just to chat to her all day long. As I carried on with my errands and jobs, I would potter about, telling her all the things I was doing and talk to her about anything and everything. Of course she didn't understand but it meant that she was familiar with the sound of my voice – the inflections and my tone – and very quickly she began to coo and garble back at me. It was quite nice to talk all day and not have somebody answer back, haha!

As the little pudding (Matt still calls her 'PuddingFace' sometimes, teehee) grew towards toddlerhood, I felt like our hearts were completely knitted together and that I could never love anything more than I love this sweet human. There is something so incredible about the way a child takes all your energy, time and spare pennies, but all you want to do is continue to give. If I could pour every drop of love out of my body and into hers, I would.

Sometimes I cuddle her tight and tell her that I will love her for ever and always. She replies, 'Mummy I love you all the day and all the night and all the conkers.' There are a lot of conkers out there, so I'm happy with that offering. That's a lot of lovin'! I know she feels my love and is aware that she is everything to me, but I always want to imprint on her the eternity of this love. That, no matter what she does or where she goes in her life, I will always see her as perfection, this cherished child of mine. I think that's the beauty of bonding; you imprint your love on each other's hearts.

That's the beauty
of bonding;
you imprint your
love on each
♡ other's hearts. ♡

Being Kind

If you have spent any time at all watching me on YouTube or reading my blog, you will know that one of my favourite things to talk about is being kind, spreading love and having a positive, proactive attitude to life. I spent the majority of my teens not feeling that way at all, but I had a total turnaround in my twenties and I wanted to write this chapter to guide those of you who might need a little bit of love and help.

A warm hug from me to you, this – a hug that you can pass on to someone else too.

Why should we exercise kindness?

Unless you live like a total hermit, whatever you do in life, you will be surrounded by people. Some are people you actively seek out (friends, lovers – ooerr! – family members) and some are people who you are obliged to exist alongside (colleagues, school/university pupils, the woman that stands behind you in the queue at the supermarket). Either way, you gots to be with the peoples and so you may as well make the very best of that.

The absolute easiest way to make the very best of this is with kindness. Before we talk about ways we can be kind, let's strip it back and look at what 'kindness' actually is.

♡ **Kindness to me is love.**

♡ **It is treating other people with a warm heart.**

♡ **It is doing good things for them, showing care and behaving towards them with a positive attitude.**

♡ **It is having their best interests at heart and only doing things that you think will benefit them.**

Sometimes it requires a bit of extra effort from you or sometimes it is hard because it doesn't directly align with exactly what you want, but I believe love is always the answer and so kindness is important.

♡ **Be kind.**

Just like you, other people are walking through their journey of life and sometimes that's thrilling and easy, and sometimes it's downright difficult. It can be hard or even impossible to tell what kind of road people are on and, in some cases, **showing a bit of kindness can make**

all the difference to another person's journey and can lead them on a better path. This might all sound like I'm talking in riddles, but what I'm trying to say is this: you don't know how crummy someone might feel. If you show them great love and kindness, you can make a really positive impact on their lives without even knowing it. **You have the power to lift someone up, to make them smile and to brighten their day.** Isn't that kind of cool? I think it is. Imagine if we all recognised this power and used it to its full potential. Imagine if every day people were looking for ways to throw kindness around like confetti and make the folk around them all kinds of happy. It would be amazing. The world would be such a wonderful place!

♡ **Kindness makes people feel loved, and secure, and appreciated, and valued.**

♡ **Loved, secure, appreciated, valued people are more likely to feel happy.**

♡ **Happy people are generally motivated and excited for life.**

Think of every single person you know or have in your life (yes, even that lady standing behind you at the checkout queue). Think about how great it would be if every single one of those people were happy and excited for life.

The repercussions of this, when you stop and think about them, are huge. We would stop focusing on the petty and pathetic things that drag us down, and instead we would look to what we can do to better the world, ourselves and our loved ones, and we'd all work more towards good, positive things. You know how businesses sometimes say 'A happy workforce is a good workforce?' They're right.

Kindness isn't just a twee thing that little old ladies practise. It's something we can all work to increase and can all see really big results from. I bet if you try, you'll surprise yourself!

Ways kindness has affected me

I feel kindness in so many different ways in my life that I thought it might be fun to share some of them with you. This way, you can have a think and see if these things are popping up in your day-to-day as well. **Often we don't notice when someone is showing us a kindness**, but when you stop and look for them, they're everywhere! A kindness doesn't have to be a deliberate act of love; it can be found in the little moments of care people show you (even when they're not obliged to).

♡   My favourite acts of kindness are the ones you don't expect. Sometimes, when I go into the London office for meetings or to pick things up, my manager Maddie (or 'Maddieger', as I like to call her) will give me a squeeze and say, 'I do love it when you're in the office.' I always feel a bit squishy in my heart when she does that, because it's one of those things that's an added extra. I was going to be there anyway, we have to spend time together because of our jobs, it's a day of work stuff, yadda yadda. But my heart squishes to know that a) I am loved and b) that I was told I am loved. It's nice. It's kind.

In turn, because of this kindness, I always take treats (usually biscuits and sweets) into the office with me, to show Maddie and the girls that I care too. Both of those things are so low key – a sweet sentiment and a packet of cookies – but they're the sorts of things that really, truly enrich a day.

♡ Another type of kindness that is always appreciated is the kindness you receive when you need it a great deal. We've all had those days where you just feel really downhearted and can't seem to drag yourself out of a thought bog. It's frustrating and demotivating, and I have found that in those moments a little bit of kindness goes a really long way.

Have you ever been having an awful day and then your phone pings with a silly picture from a friend, or your neighbour waves at you and asks how you are? Those tiny titbits of friendliness remind you that life isn't all that bad and that there are people all around who want to offer you compassion. When I think about things like that, my day doesn't seem so awful and the matter that was bothering me feels so much smaller. It's quite wonderful really.

♡ A third type of kindness is the oh-so-on-purpose type, and they're pretty freakin' cool too. You find these mostly on birthdays and on special occasions. The sort of day where friends rally round to make you feel special, and you just know they've had days or weeks of secret WhatsApp chats about their plans to please and surprise you. It's in those moments that I feel so full of love for the people around me that I cry. I'm naturally a crier but, honestly, when people go out of their way to do something sweet especially for me, I'm a goner!

♡ Then of course there are all the teeny weeny things that just help make a day a little brighter. Someone holding a lift door open for you as you run for it, your next-door neighbour putting your bin out when they see you've forgotten, a text from a friend to say 'Happy Monday', or that smiley lady in the street who picks up Darcy's toy when she sees it's been dropped and I haven't noticed. All these easily missed acts of kindness are worth looking out for. When you start noticing them, you'll want to give more of them out yourself, and so a happier world is born.

Ways you can be kind to the world in general

Now that we've looked at all the many ways kindness can be felt and how it can affect us, I thought it might be fun to suggest a few ways you could pass on the love yourself. If you do any of these, tweet me @SprinkleofGlitr and let me know. Hearing positive things never gets old and can be a real inspiration.

Being kind doesn't need to cost money or take great effort. Some of the kindest things you can do for a person or people are the simplest things.

Smile.

Have you ever walked down the road feeling really glum? I have. And then, a stranger catches your eye and smiles at you, and you almost can't help smiling back. Feels good doesn't it? Do that to more people. It takes virtually no effort and can have a really uplifting effect on their day!

Offer help.

Either at home or at work, or for a friend or neighbour. Offer to give them a little bit of help with some chores or little jobs they have. It might only take a few minutes of your time but it shows how much you care and will help them feel supported and cherished. Also, you'll win a whole heap o' brownie points!

Listen.

Sometimes all people need is an open ear to talk to. I know that when I have an issue, more often than not I want a friend to hear me out, rather than offer a solution. It's no bother at all to sit with someone whilst they pour their heart out, so make yourself available for that whenever you can. Remember, though, it's important to keep what they say confidential; they could be trusting you with a lot.

Remind.

In the hustle and bustle of life it's easy to forget that we are so cared for, so take a couple of minutes out of your day to remind the people that matter that you care about them. Maybe send a quick text or, if you have more time, call or go and see them. It's a sure-fire way to make someone super-happy.

Babysit.

For me, this is the greatest kindness. I have a hard time asking for help with my daughter, because I don't like people to ever feel like I am burdening them. So when friends or family offer to babysit I am always so grateful. If you have friends or family with little ones, offer up your babysitting services and give those tired mamas and papas a night off!

Rise above it.

Sometimes it's quite hard to be kind, especially if a person has been unfair to you or downright nasty. It can be quite the challenge to respond with a warm heart. These are the times when it's most important, though. If you can be kind in the face of negativity, you have mastered a big life skill. It's tricky but so, so worth it.

All of the above options cost no money at all. Kindness is afforded by the heart, not by the purse.

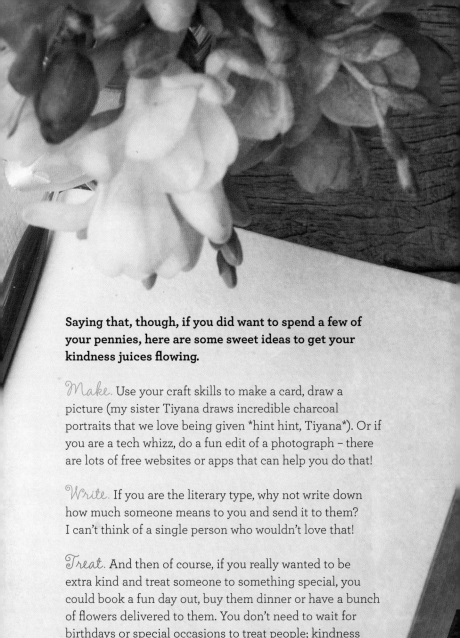

Saying that, though, if you did want to spend a few of your pennies, here are some sweet ideas to get your kindness juices flowing.

Make. Use your craft skills to make a card, draw a picture (my sister Tiyana draws incredible charcoal portraits that we love being given *hint hint, Tiyana*). Or if you are a tech whizz, do a fun edit of a photograph – there are lots of free websites or apps that can help you do that!

Write. If you are the literary type, why not write down how much someone means to you and send it to them? I can't think of a single person who wouldn't love that!

Treat. And then of course, if you really wanted to be extra kind and treat someone to something special, you could book a fun day out, buy them dinner or have a bunch of flowers delivered to them. You don't need to wait for birthdays or special occasions to treat people; kindness doesn't work to a schedule.

The main point of this chapter is to encourage you to open your heart and spread love, kindness and positivity with abundance. You can never run out of kindness and you never lose out by giving more. You can always create positivity for yourself and others, and I'm not sure I can think of anything better than that. Except maybe melted chocolate.

So, challenge yourself.

♡ **How much kindness can you give in one day?**

♡ **How many kind things can you think of to do for one person?**

♡ **How many times can you take the kind route, even when you feel so much like not taking it?**

Once you start doing these things, they become addictive and a part of day-to-day life, and with that you are spreading a sprinkle of glitter wherever you go.

Be kind.

Open your heart
and spread love,
kindness and
positivity with
abundance.

Toodlepip!

And so here we are at the end of the book, with only our 'toodlepips' left to say.

I sincerely hope you have loved reading this book as much as I loved putting it together. Writing it has been both enjoyable and cathartic, and my aim has been for you to gain something positive from each section. I hope I've helped you in some way or that you've had a quiet LOL at some of my faux pas.

SINCERELY

As you tuck this little book away on your shelf or in your drawer, please remember that in each and every page I have sprinkled my love for you, and if ever you are feeling a bit blue or in need of a pick me up, I'm here. If ever you are unsure or if you are having a cringe-y day, remember all of my awkward encounters and know that, like me, you can learn and grow from each one. In the end, it will always be alright.

Walk through your life with a smile, a glad heart and a positive attitude, and you'll never go far wrong.

Thank you for being a part of Sprinkle of Glitter — you mean the world to me.

Big, big sparkly hugs and all the glittery kisses,

Louise x X x

Thank yous

This book would never have been turned from sparkly little thoughts into the colourful pages you hold in your hands without the diligent work of a fantastic team.

I would like to thank **Maddie**, **Natalie** and **Dom**, my wonderful management team at **Gleam Futures**, who have always been so supportive. Maddie for laughing at my often rubbish jokes, telling me I was doing a good job on the days I fretted and for actually crying happy tears on the day we saw the mock-up of the designs. She is one of the most important ladies in my life and I don't know where I'd be without her constant care and guiding hands. Thank you also to Natalie for her incredible patience when I didn't read her emails and for never, ever shouting at me when I sent my chapters in late. Without Natalie's persistent nudging, I'm not sure where we'd be (probably somewhere around Chapter 3 still!).

I'd like to thank all the incredible team at **Simon & Schuster** for being brave enough to let me write a book with them! Most especially, **Abigail Bergstrom** for being the most chilled-out (to my face, teehee) editor a gal could hope for; **Jo Whitford**, my copy-editor, who I'm sure saw more spelling errors than any copy-editor ever should; **Corinna Farrow**, my super designer, who has put so much love and magic onto every single page; and **Emma Harrow** and **Isabel Prodger**, the publicists.

To my family and friends – thank you a million squillion. Although it was me who tippy-tap-typed each word, it was them pushing me on and encouraging each chapter, and without them I wouldn't have managed. **Matt** and **Darcy** – thank you for understanding when I locked myself away for hours and weekends at a time to get this done. I will always be grateful for all the dinners

Matt cooked and delivered to my office (and by 'office', I mean the bed that I sat in with my laptop for most of this book, hahaha!). To my chummy **Zoe**, for always being such a calming force when everything got a bit stressful and I did a little cry about how much there was to do – thank you for your practical tips and endless phone calls, I love ya. To **Jack** and **Ben** – thank you for always encouraging me to speak my mind and to have the courage to try things I don't think I can do. To **Hazel** – the biggest thank you for never begrudging the times I put the book before our adventures and cancelled on you, you are a good woman. To **Clare**, who has celebrated each little milestone with sweet cards, glasses of bubbly and a cheeky takeaway here and there – thank you for always sharing my happiness. And finally, thank you to **Dad** and lovely **Tina** for your boundless parental love, and to Dad, who said, 'It will be a bestseller, I know it!', just because he's my dad.

It is the author who is credited most for writing a book, but for every 'well done' or congratulatory high five I receive for this little treasure trove of words, I am sharing each one with these people, who are so dear to my heart and who have been everything I needed and more along this journey.

Picture Credits

A big thank you to Liane Payne for invaluable picture research.

© Louise Pentland: cover, 2, 9, 11, 46, 47, 48, 49, 50, 67, 82, 100, 109, 110, 111, 113, 115, 117, 118, 120, 121, 122, 123, 166, 172, 194, 234, 236, 237

© dailymixtv: 115

© Abigail Bergstrom: 228

© Corinna Farrow: 2, 55, 111, 126, 186, 187

© Getty Images/PhotoDisc: 2, 8, 9, 10, 11, 40, 45, 61, 72, 73, 74, 75, 76, 77, 78, 79, 96, 97, 106, 107, 128, 142, 143, 144, 145, 176, 177, 180, 181, 187, 193, 224, 225, endpapers; Stockdisc: 77, 194, 195

© iStock.com: cover, 1, 3, 24, 25, 26, 27, 34, 40, 41, 46, 47, 52, 57, 84, 85, 86, 90, 91, 92, 93, 98, 99, 101, 112, 120, 121

© Veer.com: 90, 93

All additional images © Shutterstock.com (Luciano Mortula/shutterstock.com 196; Pedrosala/shutterstock.com 200; Hadrian/shutterstock.com 166, 167)